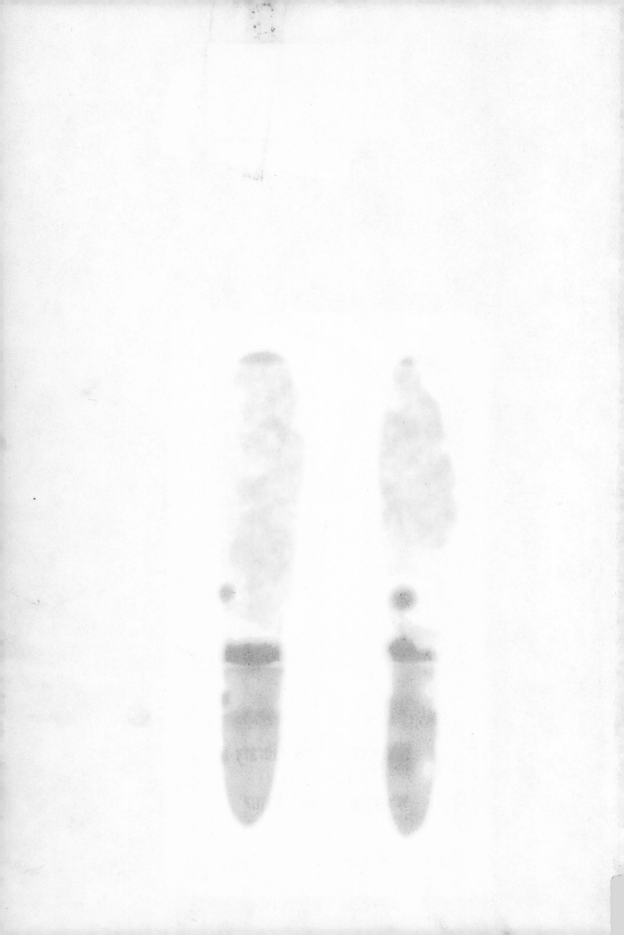

The Art of
PAPIER MÂCHÉ

Also by John B. Kenny

THE COMPLETE BOOK OF POTTERY MAKING
CERAMIC SCULPTURE
CERAMIC DESIGN

The Art of
PAPIER MÂCHÉ

CARLA AND JOHN B. KENNY

WITH DRAWINGS AND PHOTOGRAPHS BY THE AUTHORS

CHILTON BOOK COMPANY
PHILADELPHIA   NEW YORK   LONDON

ACKNOWLEDGMENTS

to Jay D. de Armstrong and Alicia S. de Ramirez
who helped in our research with paper mash,

to Lala V. de Valera who taught us how to create with bread paste,

to the Norcross Company who gave permission
to use their special gift wrapping papers,

to students of the High School of Art and Design of New York City who assisted in the
taking of color photographs, and

to all of our friends who were generous with
criticisms and encouragement,

our sincerest thanks,

THE AUTHORS

v

CONTENTS

Materials. Paste. Types of paper. Making a box. Patterns. Making a lid with a knob. Drying. Warping. Finishing. Decorating with twine.

Ingredients. A recipe. Beating paper pulp. Mixing mash. Modeling in pulp. Modeling in mash. White mash. Ready-mix mash. Using an armature. Drying mash. Applying mash to paper construction. Printing designs with vegetables and tempera paint. Gesso. A recipe.

CHAPTER

PHOTO SERIES

BLACK AND WHITE PLATES

COLOR PLATES

(Color insert is between pages 80 and 81)

INTRODUCTION

Wonderful things have been done by the manufacturers of paper—so many wonderful things, in fact, that we have grown accustomed to their excellence and take for granted the great variety of papers that serves us in so many ways. Recently, however, we have become aware that this material is beautiful as well as useful.

In other parts of the world artists have been creating things out of paper for a long time: intricately folded designs in Japan, elaborate cutouts in Scandinavia and Central Europe, piñatas in Mexico. The Chinese started it all about 2,000 years ago when they discovered the secret of making paper. Not long after that they began to use their new discovery to produce artistic cutouts, kites and paper dragons. Next, they mashed the paper and made more solid things—boxes, trays, figurines, etc.—and so began the art of *papier mâché*.

The craft had a surge of popularity in Europe in the early part of the 18th century at a time when the printing presses were busy turning out posters and the first crude newspapers. Paper making machinery had not yet been invented, so even street bulletins were

xiii

printed on handmade paper. The French, seeking a method for using their discarded posters, chopped up the waste paper, made a mash, added glue, then formed it into snuff boxes and other objects. The Germans, too, became fascinated by the possibility of making useful things out of waste material and built a papier mâché factory in Berlin in 1765.

Time has proven that papier mâché can have lasting beauty as well as utility. Toys, trays, picture frames, even pieces of furniture, made of this material 200 years ago are still usable and just as attractive as they were the day when the artist finished the design and applied the final coat of lacquer.

It is in Mexico that craftsmen have the most fun with paper. They use it for every festive occasion. Just before Easter, papier mâché Judases are loaded with fireworks and then blown up amid shouts of delight, and no Christmas or birthday would be complete without a *piñata*.

The bases of piñatas are large, fragile earthenware pots on which bits of colored paper are pasted to make all shorts of shapes—stars, rockets, animals, birds, people, giant flowers. At fiesta time a piñata is loaded with candy and small toys and suspended from above while blindfolded children try to hit it with a stick. When a youngster succeeds, the pot breaks; the goodies shower downward on the young merry makers. The piñata, alas, is no more. Like the Judas, its fulfillment comes at the moment of its destruction.

Today the artistic possibilities of papier mâché have been rediscovered by artists, by interior decorators, by fashion designers. The material has found its way into sophisticated, modern decor; it is used for fashionable jewelry and accessories—even for dresses.

As a craft material for people with the urge to create, papier mâché is ideal. It is easy to work with, responds readily to the touch. It can be used to make larger-than-life sculpture, or to fashion rings for the fingers or the ears. It gives an opportunity to explore and to try different methods of manipulation. It can be used for conventional shapes or ones that are way out, completely different from anything ever made before. It encourages wild, mad, uninhibited use of color.

And it is cheap! (What a blessing to hear that word today.) No equipment to install, no tools to buy (everything needed is at hand in the kitchen). Pastes and pigments cost little, scrap paper is free.

So—let's get busy. Bring that stack of last week's newspapers from the basement, the advertising circulars that went into the waste basket this morning. Let's see if we can make something beautiful out of something that was thrown away.

The Art of
PAPIER MÂCHÉ

1

CONSTRUCTING WITH PAPER

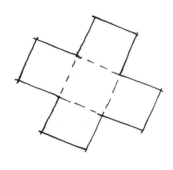

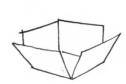

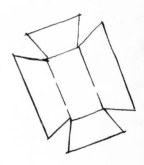

MAKING something out of any material, be it wood, metal, clay or paper, is first a problem in mechanics. One must learn the tricks of manipulating the material. Second, and this is the more important part, it is a problem in design.

The easiest way to make a shape out of paper or cardboard is to cut a pattern and fold it. Cubes and rectangular boxes can be made this way and so can a number of geometric solids that have flat sides. Cylindrical shapes can be rolled and so can cones. Spherical forms are a bit more complicated. We will talk about them in chapter 4. For our first construction in paper we'll make a rectangular box with a lid.

MATERIALS

We shall need newspaper, corrugated cardboard (the kind used for grocery cartons), a bit of cellophane tape and paste. The best paste for this work is wheat paste, the kind used for hanging wallpaper. It comes in dry powder form and can be bought in hardware stores or art supply shops. It is mixed in the ratio of one tablespoon of powder to one cup of water. A good way to mix the paste is to use a jar with a screw-on lid. Put the water in the jar, add the dry powder, fasten the lid and shake vigorously for ten seconds. This will produce a smooth, creamy paste free from lumps. If you prefer a thinner paste, add a little water and shake again. Mix only as much paste as is needed for one session; it is best to start each day's work with freshly mixed paste.

At times glue must be used instead of paste. The best for papier mâché work is the white synthetic glue which comes in liquid form in plastic containers.

Some papier mâché artists like to make their own paste by mixing flour and water, a process we have found not worth the trouble. But if you want to make your own, a recipe is given in chapter 13.

PHOTO SERIES 1
Rectangular box with lid

1. The pattern has been cut out of a piece of corrugated cardboard. The lines on which the pattern is to be folded have been scored with a blunt pointed instrument (a closed pair of scissors).

This pattern will make a box 5¾ inches long, 3¾ inches wide and 2½ inches high, a convenient size for cigarettes or candy. These proportions may be varied, of course, to suit different purposes.

A piece of cardboard 6½ inches by 4½ inches has been cut out for the lid. A ⅜-inch strip, 18 inches long, will be used to form a flange on the underside of the lid.

2. The sides of the box have been folded up and fastened with cellophane tape. Now newspaper is pasted on.

A strip of newspaper 5⅜ inches wide by 23 inches long (the full width of a tabloid sheet) has been dampened and given a liberal coating of paste. The box has been placed in position so that the ends of the strip can be wrapped around the sides of the box, covering the outside and the inside surfaces of the sides and bottom. Care must be taken to brush the newspaper firmly so that no air pockets are left between it and the cardboard.

When this strip is in place, another strip 3⅜ inches wide will be dampened and fastened in similar fashion so that it will cover both surfaces of the bottom and the ends of the box.

Note: In most of our work we shall not cut paper, but tear it. For a rectangular box, however, cutting the paper makes the work go more quickly.

3. Another strip of dampened newspaper 4 inches wide is wrapped around the four sides of the box, then folded over so that it seals all sides and corners as well as the top edges. Again, plenty of paste is used and care is taken to press the paper firmly in place.

Steps 2 and 3 are repeated until all surfaces of the box, both inside and outside, are covered with three layers of newspaper.

4. The flange is fastened onto the underside of the lid with strips of damp newspaper and paste. As soon as this step is completed, the lid must be tried in place to make sure it will fit.

5. Some type of knob or handle seems called for. A piece of newspaper was rolled into a cone and pasted; now it is cut as shown.

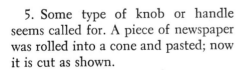

3

6. The cone is flattened. The strips at the wide end are folded over and pasted to form a knob.

7. Pasting the knob in place. Diagonal lines were drawn to help in centering the knob. The corners of the lid have been cut round.

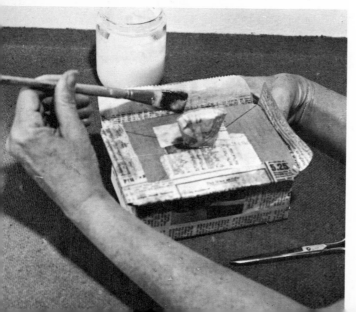

8. Sealing the edges of the lid. Strips of newspaper have been pasted to the underside of the lid; now they are being folded over the top rim and pasted flat.

4

9. The construction of the box and the lid has been completed. They are ready to be put aside to dry.

DRYING

Our box will dry overnight if it is propped up in some way so that air can circulate freely around all sides. The drying process can be hastened by standing it in strong sunlight, on a warm radiator or in an oven. It may be baked for a few minutes at 250°F., but a better plan is to use a lower heat (150°F.) and leave the box in the oven somewhat longer. DON'T put work in the oven and forget it. Remove it as soon as it is dry. Prop the door of the oven open slightly during the drying process.

WARPING

Shapes made of paper and paste have a tendency to warp as they dry. In some forms, slight warping does not matter, but a box should be square and the lid should fit properly. While the box is damp, it must be pressed gently until it has the right shape, then held in that shape until it is dry.

10. The box and the lid drying in a warm oven. A rubber band around the box helps to keep it square. Pieces of light cardboard (the kind used for facial tissue boxes) have been folded and placed at the corners of the box to keep the rubber band from cutting into it. Stones placed on the lid will make it dry flat.

5

FINISHING

One of the joys of working with paper is that we have such a wide choice of ways to finish the things we make. The box, for example, can be sandpapered when it is dry, then painted with any of many different kinds of paint. Or it can be painted without any preliminary sanding. The rougher surface produced that way will give the finished article quite a different appearance.

Rectangles about ¾ of an inch by 1½ inches torn from newspaper and pasted in rows on the surface of a paper construction produce a pattern which is effective.

11. Pasting paper rectangles in rows so that they overlap slightly.

12. When the box and its lid were dry, they were given a base coat of water-soluble wall paint. (This and other materials used are described more fully in chapter 13.) After the base coat was dry, the work was painted with a mixture of evaporated milk and powdered instant coffee.

6

MILK

A hard semi-mat surface (not waterproof) results when milk, either regular or evaporated, is brushed over a paper construction. When powdered instant coffee is added to evaporated milk in sufficient quantity to make a creamy paste, the mixture, when painted on the box, gives it a warm "café au lait" tone which accents the modeling of the surface and makes the pattern of the rectangles clearly visible.

13. When the milk and coffee mixture was dry, a design was painted on the box with poster colors. As a final step to give the work a durable surface, it was given two coats of clear lacquer.

Instead of painting directly on a box, designs can be painted on paper, then pasted on. Or printed designs can be cut out and mounted on the work (montage). Other things can be used for ornamentation —for example, string. Here, another box is decorated by this method.

14. A box and its lid are given a coating of white glue.

15. Lightweight twine is glued to the box in a decorative pattern. Two bowls are used. The one at the upper left contains water, the other glue. The twine is first moistened, then drawn through the glue, and then pressed on the design which has been sketched on the box.

16. The finished box. The design was painted with tempera colors and given two coats of varnish, the second brushed on after the first coat was thoroughly dry.

1. Papier mâché cig-
arette box, match
box and ash tray
from Kashmir

Papier mâché boxes can be made just the right size and shape for the things they are to contain (note the box for chessmen shown in color plate 1). Since they are decorative, they need not be hidden in closets, but can be left in full view to be used and enjoyed.

Making boxes this way is a form of carpentry, using paper and cardboard instead of wood; scissors and knife in place of a saw; and brush and paste in place of hammer and nails. These boxes are paper, but *not* papier mâché.

The possibilities of paper go far beyond those of carpentry. When paper has been beaten into a pulp and made into a mash, it can be shaped into forms impossible to achieve with hammer and saw.

9

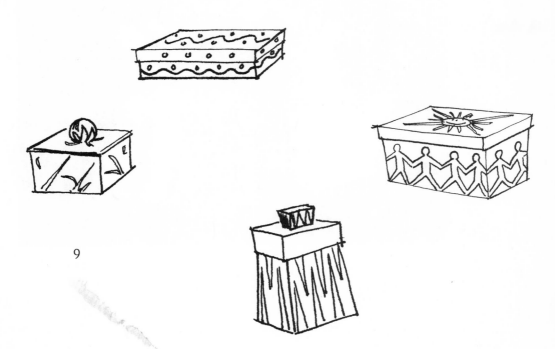

2
PAPER
MASH

Papier mâché, literally translated, means chewed up paper. Paper which has been soaked in water, then beaten into a pulp, can be squeezed into forms which, when dry, will hold their shape. Some

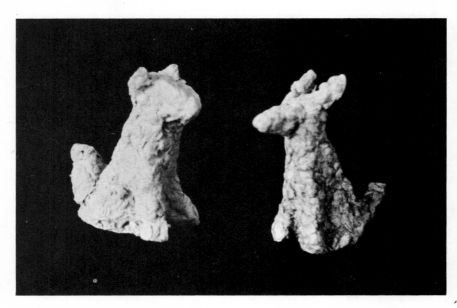

2. Test figures

of the projects shown in later chapters were made of paper pulp with nothing else added (see photo series 14 and 31). However, paper pulp alone is not suitable for most papier mâché work. Other ingredients must be added.

There is no single formula for papier mâché. Most artists have their own, some of them jealously guarded secrets. Among many mixtures which we have tried, the best results have been obtained from the following recipe:

Recipe for one quart of mash

4 sheets of full-sized newspaper (16 pages)
2 tablespoons whiting
2 tablespoons white glue
1 tablespoon linseed oil (either raw or boiled)
2 tablespoons wheat paste flour
2 drops oil of wintergreen or oil of cloves

PHOTO SERIES 2
Preparing paper mash

1. *Tearing and soaking.* We start by tearing the newspaper into pieces no larger than one inch square. This paper has a grain running from the top to the bottom of the page; it is easier to tear long, narrow strips in this direction.

The pieces of paper are put into a container, covered with water and allowed to soak overnight.

2. *Beating.* The soaked paper has been put into a large cooking vessel and boiled for twenty minutes in two quarts of water to loosen the fibers. A metal whisk is used to whip the paper into a pulp.

Note: A power mixer or an electric blender will make the whipping process quicker and easier. No harm will be done to a blender if plenty of water is used. Stirring in the blender for five seconds will produce a good workable mash; longer blending will produce a finer mash with a more even texture. (When power mixers are used, it is not necessary to boil the paper first.)

3. *Straining*. The paper pulp is dipped into a strainer which is then tapped several times to shake out some of the water.

4. *Paper pulp*. After it has been strained, the pulp will form a soft, wet lump which can be held in the hand as shown. This lump is still more than 90% water. It may be compressed between the two hands so that more water is forced out, but be careful not to squeeze too hard so that the lump becomes tough and unworkable.

5. *Mixing*. The pulp, still quite wet and soft, has been put into a bowl. Two heaping tablespoons of whiting have been sprinkled into the pulp with two tablespoons of white glue and one tablespoon of linseed oil. A few drops of oil of wintergreen are added and the mixture is stirred with a large spoon. An electric egg beater can be used to stir the mash, but a blender should NOT be used at this stage (too difficult to clean).

When the mash has been thoroughly mixed, two tablespoons of dry wheat paste should be sprinkled in and the mixture stirred again. When the mix is thoroughly stirred, it is ready for use.

The quantities mentioned here can be varied considerably. More glue makes a stronger finished product; more whiting makes a whiter, denser mash. If this mixture is too watery when all the ingredients have been stirred in, more wheat paste can be added to take up the extra moisture and make the mash creamier.

The glue and the paste serve as binders. Whiting (calcium carbonate) acts as a filler; it improves the color of the finished product and adds density. Linseed oil is an extender; it makes the mash easier to work with and also gives the finished product extra toughness. Oil of cloves or oil of wintergreen acts as a preservative, preventing the mash from becoming sour. Oil of wintergreen or oil of cloves can be purchased at a drug store. All of the other materials can be bought at a hardware store.

Almost any scrap paper can be made into mash. Newspaper is easiest to use if the pulp must be beaten by hand. When a blender is available, heavier types of paper—circulars, bond paper, business correspondence, etc.—can be used. Colored papers add interesting flecks. Try some experiments—an old road map, for example—or airmail envelopes with stamps. (Don't boil colored papers.)

WHITE MASH

Artists who work with a white porcelain-like finish make a mash out of white paper napkins and paper towels. White toilet paper of good quality makes an excellent mash. One roll is enough for two quarts of mash. Where whiteness is important, raw linseed oil should be used.

READY-MIX MASH

A prepared papier mâché flour can be bought from art supply dealers. This, when mixed with water, is ready for use. It costs about one dollar a pound. For anyone who plans to make a few small articles, this ready-mix flour is quite satisfactory. However, for larger or more extensive work, it could prove expensive. The true artist in papier mâché prefers to make his own.

Now that we have made a batch of paper mash, let's make something with it. We have a bowl of a grayish mixture, quite wet and soft. It can be pressed into shapes and smoothed with a knife or a spoon. It has some of the characteristics of modeling clay, but not

13

all. If we try to form it into an intricate shape, we find it much too soft. We could squeeze out most of the water, but when we do that we find it is no longer easy to manipulate, but becomes obstinate and lumpy. We can, however, model a simple shape if we use an armature to support the mash.

PHOTO SERIES 3
A papier mâché horse

1. Pipe cleaners have been twisted into an armature for the figure of a small animal. After the armature was shaped it was dipped in glue and allowed to dry. The glue makes the armature stronger and prevents the pipe cleaner wire from rusting and making ugly stains.

Mash is applied with the fingers and squeezed into shape on the armature. A piece cut from the core of a toilet paper roll is a temporary support.

2. The modeling completed. The figure will now be set aside to dry.

3. The finished horse. Mane and tail are made of cord dipped in ink and then in glue. The eyes and hoofs are painted with tempera.

14

A TURNTABLE

During the making of the horse, the work stood on a small plastic turntable. This device is very helpful in sculpture; it allows the work to be turned frequently and viewed from different angles as modeling progresses. Such turntables, quite inexpensive, can be bought from art supply dealers.

DRYING MASH

Some interesting changes take place in mash as it dries and shrinks. A surface that was smooth when wet will be bumpy when it is dry. When mash has lost most of its moisture, but is not yet entirely dry, it becomes more plastic. In this state it can be shaped more easily and surfaces can be made smoother.

A figure like the little horse we just made will dry overnight. Strong sunlight hastens the drying process. Or we may use an oven. About fifteen minutes in an oven temperature of 150°F. should be enough to dry a small figure, but watch the drying process closely. You may wish to take the object out of the oven before it is thoroughly dry and work on it, then put it back. The oven door should be propped open slightly during drying.

Be careful not to scorch your work. A good safety device is to place the object in the oven on several layers of dry newspaper. When the newspaper gets too hot, the odor will warn you that it is time to turn off the oven.

Now let's see how mash can be used on a box like the one we made in chapter 1.

PHOTO SERIES 4
Applying mash

1. Before mash is applied to an object, the surface must be brushed with thin paste or diluted glue (one part water and one part glue).

2. A layer of mash is pressed on the lid with a paring knife.

3. Blotting up excess moisture with a paper towel.

4. Smoothing. The box has been in a warm oven (150°F.) with the door propped open for 20 minutes. The mash has lost most of its moisture but is not yet dry. In this state it can be made quite smooth by drawing a knife blade over the surface.

5. When the mash has dried completely, it can be smoothed with sandpaper (medium or coarse) or with a coarse wood rasp.

16

Gesso

We must learn how to make and use another material, one with which the artists of the Renaissance prepared surfaces for their paintings. As with paper mash, there are many different formulas for gesso. We have had best results with a mixture of whiting, glue, linseed oil and water prepared as follows:

> *Recipe for gesso.* Sprinkle two tablespoons of whiting into a container of water and allow it to settle. *Don't stir!* After it has stood for several minutes, carefully pour off all of the excess water. Add one tablespoon of white glue and one teaspoon of linseed oil (raw or boiled) and stir thoroughly. The mixture should have the consistency of thick cream. If it is too thin, sprinkle in more whiting and stir until smooth.

Gesso is excellent for brushing on papier mâché. It seals pores, covers rough spots and dries with a hard white surface, just right for a painting base. It can be sanded before painting if necessary.

6. The box has been given a coat of gesso and allowed to dry overnight.

7. Another interesting way to decorate a papier mâché object is by vegetable printing. Carrots, potatoes and other vegetables, cut and notched as shown, make dies with which designs can be stamped. Here tempera color is brushed onto a cut potato. When this is pressed against the surface of the box it will print a design like the one shown on the paper napkin.

8. Potato and carrot prints on the box.

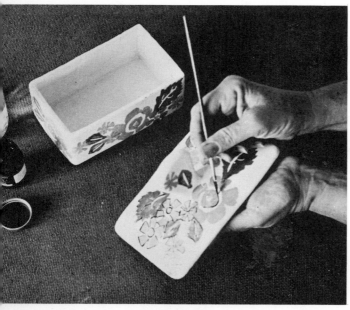

9. Outlining printed designs with black tempera.

10. The finished box. It has been sprayed with four coats of lacquer.

18

3
CYLINDERS

Tʜᴇ cylinder is a basic shape in paper construction. Here are the steps in making a cylindrical box with a lid, using a glass jar as a form on which to shape the cylinder.

PHOTO SERIES 5
A cylindrical box with lid

1. A piece of newspaper is rolled around a quart jar. No paste is used at this point. A circle with triangular notches has been cut to cover the base.

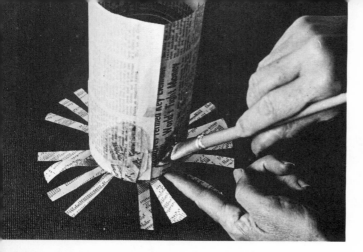

2. The paper wraparound is held in place by a bit of cellophane tape. The base is fastened in place by pasting the tabs to the side of the wraparound. There is no paste between the paper and the glass jar; the jar must be able to move freely when it is time to remove it.

3. More layers of newspaper are applied. These are pasted to the original wraparound. Another piece is fastened over the base.

4. Trimming the top edge.

20

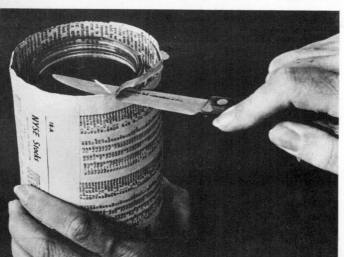

5. More strips of paper are pasted over the bottom, and larger pieces are wrapped around the side. This process will continue until the wall has been built up to a thickness of almost ⅛ inch. The jar is still inside the cylinder.

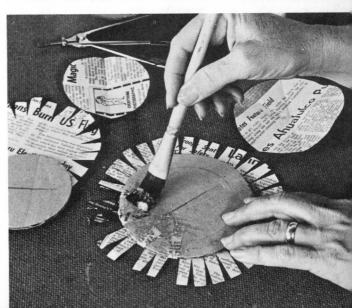

6. Binding the top edge. The wall now has the desired thickness. A piece of kraft paper (heavy grocery bag) has been torn at one edge to form tabs. The jar was removed from inside the cylinder, the kraft paper strip was pasted at the top of the cylinder. Here the tabs are being folded over and pasted in place. This step completes construction of the cylindrical box.

The jar must be put back inside and allowed to remain there while the cylinder dries.

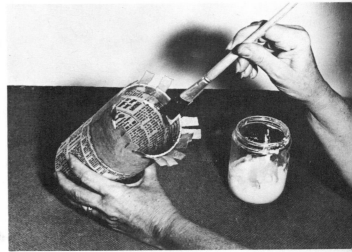

7. Making the lid. Two circles have been cut from corrugated cardboard. The larger has a diameter ½ inch greater than that of the box. (The lid should have a slight overhang.) The smaller circle has a diameter ⅛ inch less than the inside diameter of the cylinder. This will be pasted to the underside of the lid to serve as a flange, assuring proper fit. Here the larger circle is being covered with newspaper.

8. Completing the covering of the larger circle. When covering cardboard this way, an equal number of layers of newspaper must be pasted to each side to reduce warping.

9. A knob for the lid. The smaller circle has been fastened to the underside. (It cannot be seen in this photo.) A cone for a knob has been rolled out of newspaper, tabs have been cut at the edges and the cone is being pasted in place on the lid. A toothpick was pushed through the center of each circle to help in centering the knob.

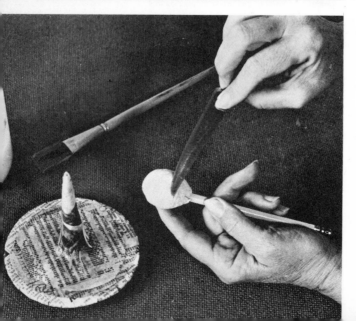

10. A ball of mash is pressed into shape over the point of a pencil. This will be fastened to the top of the cone.

22

11. Putting the ball of mash on the end of the cone.

12. While the ball was wet it was squeezed into a flat-topped shape and mash was applied to the sides of the cone to give a more pleasing contour. Here we see another way of using mash by rolling a layer. A circle the size of the box lid was drawn on newspaper. A pancake of mash is being rolled between two pieces of newspaper. A bottle is used as a rolling pin. A circle the size of the lid was drawn on the top sheet of paper before the rolling was started.

13. Scissors have been used to cut out the two sheets of paper with the mash between them. One of the layers of paper is peeled away from the mash.

23

14. With the top sheet of paper still in place, the layer of mash is applied to the lid. (The lid was given a thin coating of glue first.)

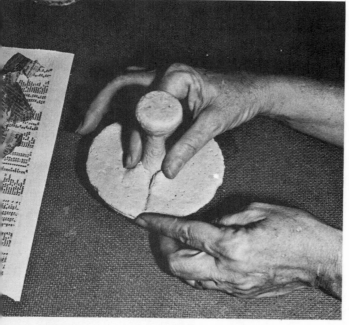

15. The remaining layer of newspaper has been peeled away and the mash is fastened onto the lid.

16. Finishing the surface of the lid with a knife and spoon. A damp sponge is kept nearby so that these two modeling tools can be frequently cleaned.

24

17. Rolling a layer of mash to be applied to the side and base of the cylinder. Here a rolling pin is used and the mash is rolled directly on a piece of newspaper without a covering layer.

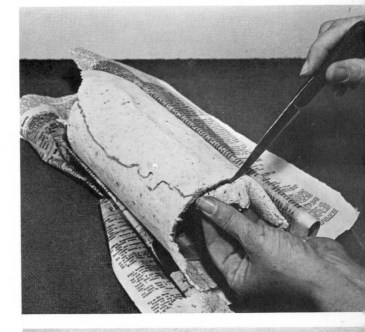

18. The mash has been wrapped around the side of the cylinder and the newspaper has been peeled away. Excess mash is cut away from the top edge of the cylinder.

19. Smoothing the mash over the base.

25

20. Rolling on dry newspaper to make the cylinder smooth and true.

21. Planning a decoration for the box. Designs are drawn on paper with felt markers, then wrapped around the cylinder and held in place by rubber bands so that the effectiveness of the design may be studied. It is a simple matter to try out many different designs in this way. When a good design is achieved, it can be reproduced by painting it directly on the cylinder, or paper bearing the design can be pasted onto the side of the box. (The markers used should be permanent color.)

In the background is a box with another decorative scheme tried out— a montage of playing cards.

22. Instead of drawing designs we may use decorative wrapping papers. Here a number of gayly colored papers are studied. At the right and left are pieces of paper that have been cut and wrapped around jars so that we can see how they would look if applied to the cylinder. The design in the lower center is not on paper; it is a painting on a piece of bark of the amate tree, a type of art produced by some of the Indians of Mexico.

23. Here is another cylindrical box. A wrapping paper with designs from old tobacco labels has been pasted on it. The lid of the box was painted with black acrylic water paint. The knob and portions of the design of the lid were painted with bronze powder (pale gold) mixed with clear lacquer. A liquid plastic lacquer is being sprayed on the box and the lid.

Three completed cylindrical boxes are shown in color plate 3.

The type of plastic lacquer used for spraying on boxes such as these may be either a high-gloss or mat. For a more durable finish, several coats of lacquer should be sprayed on with intervals for drying between successive coats.

When pasting paper on a box, the surfaces of the box should be given a coating of paste. The paper should also be brushed with paste and allowed to stand for a few minutes, then given another coating of paste and wrapped around the box. A paper towel should be used to rub the paper firmly against the box, pushing any air bubbles from under the paper.

If the design to be pasted on the box is not printed, but is original art work (like the bark painting), it should be sprayed with two coats of lacquer before paste is brushed on the back. This will prevent the colors from smearing or running.

In our construction of the cylinder, and in the box we made in chapter 1, we used large pieces of newspaper. For most papier mâché work it is better to use small pieces, and these should always be torn, not cut. Newspaper is good for the first coat. Kraft paper (brown paper bag) is good for the second coat; it is strong and the change in color makes it possible to be sure that each layer is complete. For larger work where four or five coats are needed, alternate newspaper and kraft paper.

For the final coat, unless a surface like that on the box shown in picture 12 of photo series 1 is desired, it is good to use a high grade white toilet paper. This models itself readily to contours and dries with a more even surface.

27

4
DOMED
SHAPES

Shapes which cannot be made by cutting and folding or by rolling have to be shaped over a form that serves as a mold. Here are the steps.

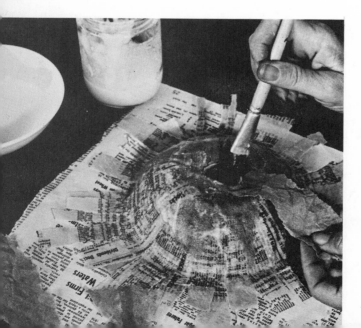

PHOTO SERIES 6
A *pencil holder*

1. A bowl such as the one shown at upper left has been wrapped with a piece of damp newspaper *without paste*. Then strips of damp newspaper with paste were laid over the entire surface. Here, after one layer of newspaper strips has been completed, a second layer of brown kraft paper is applied. This process will be continued until at least four layers of paper have been built up.

2. Trimming the edge. The work has dried overnight.

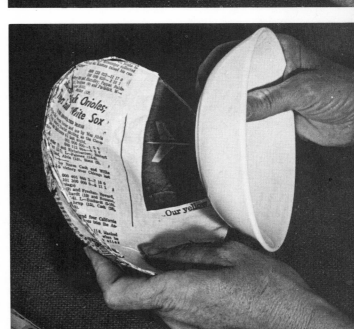

3. The bowl is removed. We now have a paper shape resembling a half sphere.

4. What happens if we roll four cones of newspaper and fasten them in place as the legs of some strange animal?

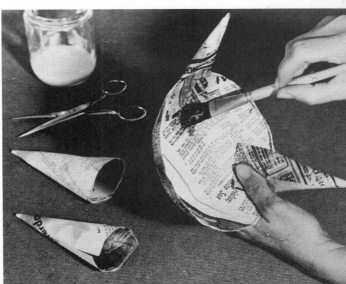

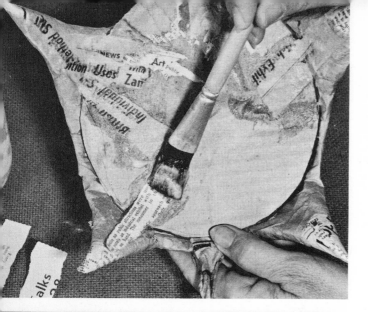

5. An elliptical shape cut from corrugated cardboard is fastened in place to form the belly of our little beast.

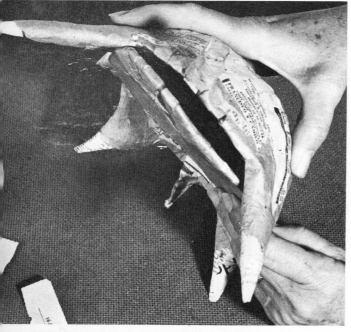

6. The edge of the cardboard that forms the bottom protrudes slightly to make an under lip. A small cone has been rolled to form a tail and a short cylinder forms a snout.

7. Newspaper ears are added.

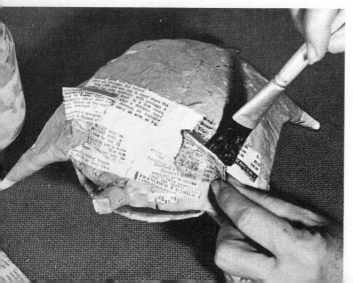

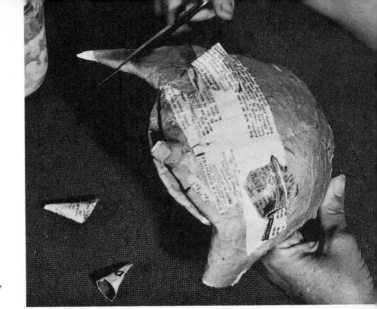

8. The legs seem too long, so they are trimmed to size.

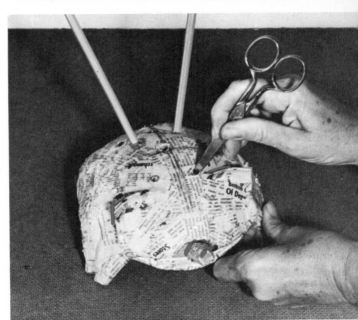

9. The surface has been given another coat of newspaper. Now perforations are made to hold pencils. Our animal turns out to be a porcupine.

10. The surface was brushed with glue; now mash is applied. Pencils are placed in the holes during this operation so that the holes won't be filled up.

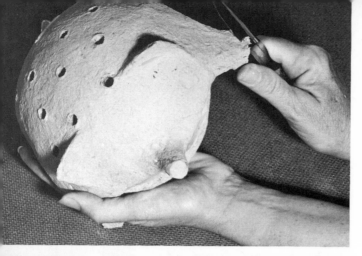

11. The mash has dried. Now the figure can be carved easily with a knife. Edges of the legs are trimmed down.

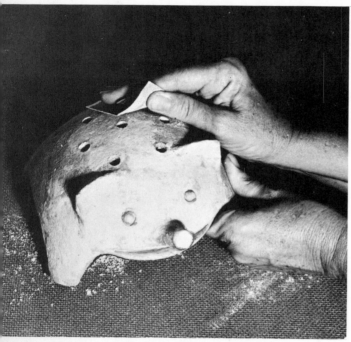

12. Sandpapering the animal. (His name is Porky Pencilpine.) Eyes were made by pressing two tiny balls of mash in place.

13. Porky has been given a coat of flat acrylic paint (pink). Now he is being decorated with twine and glue, the method used on the box in chapter 1.

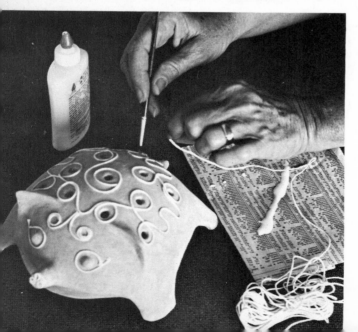

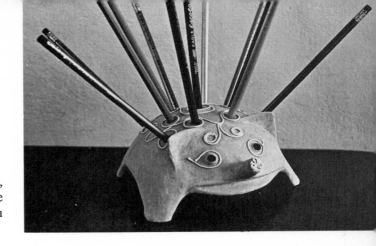

14. Porky Pencilpine is completed, ready to stand on a desk to serve people who "can never find a pencil when they need one."

In making Porky Pencilpine we did some paper construction first with strips of newspaper, kraft paper and paste, then applied a thin layer of mash. The paper construction was not absolutely necessary; when skill has been acquired in working with mash, the mash may be applied directly to a form, provided a piece of paper is wrapped around the form first so that the mash does not stick to the form. Here are the steps:

PHOTO SERIES 7
Two domed shapes to make an owl

1. This time two bowls are used. Damp newspaper is wrapped around the bowls first as a separater, then mash is applied directly as shown here. The mash must be patted into an even layer a little more than ⅛ inch thick over the entire surface of the bowl.

2. Two shells have been formed and dried. A piece of coat hanger has been cut and bent as shown to make a pair of legs. Now the coat hanger is fastened to the inside of one shell with paper and paste.

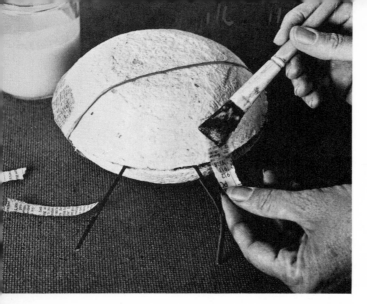

3. The two shells are held together with a rubber band while short, narrow strips of damp newspaper are pasted over the joint.

4. Making feet out of mash. To provide stability, the feet are weighted with pebbles placed inside the mash as it is shaped.

5. The feet have dried and hardened; the owl is able to stand while the shape is completed by adding mash. Large eyes are formed with marbles as pupils.

34

6. The completed owl. The colors used here were tempera paints. After they had dried, the owl was sprayed with three coats of lacquer.

Many interesting things can be made by shaping mash over bowls. Even more exciting objects can be created if, instead of using bowls, we use balloons. The next chapter tells how.

35

5

BALLOONS

WHEN domed shapes are formed over bowls, only a portion of a sphere can be made at one time. A complete globe can be made if, instead of using bowls, the paper and mash are shaped over a balloon. Here is how it is done:

3. Bonbon or flower dish made of mash pressed over a balloon end

PHOTO SERIES 8
Pasting paper over a balloon

1. Strips of damp newspaper are pasted over the entire surface of a large balloon. (It is not necessary to put any oil on the balloon first, and no separating layer is needed.)

2. After a layer of newspaper was completed, a second layer was pasted over the balloon using brown paper bag (kraft) paper. Here another layer of newspaper is pasted on. A bowl holds the work in position.

Building a form over a balloon this way is a lot of fun. At some stage in the process it will seem that the balloon is leaking air and becoming deflated. This is because the wet paper and paste make the surface of the balloon cold and the air inside contracts so that the balloon loses volume and the surface of the work starts to shrivel. When this happens, put the work into a warm oven (but with the heat off) for a few minutes. This will dry the paper layer on the surface and at the same time expand the air in the balloon so that the form resumes its full rounded character. *But watch out!* If the oven is too hot, the air inside will expand to the point where the balloon will burst through the paper shell and the work will be ruined.

37

3. It looks as if we are making another animal. Legs are being attached. This time the legs are made of the cardboard cores of toilet paper rolls. Two cores make four legs. Each is cut diagonally in the center and then the two legs so formed are fastened to the body with strips of damp newspaper.

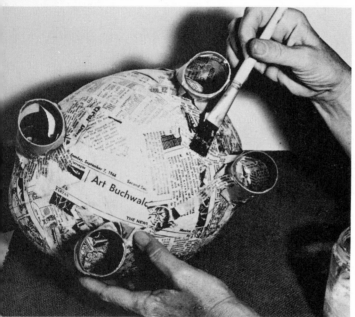

4. Completing the attaching of the legs. The openings at the bottom of the feet will be sealed with pieces of newspaper.

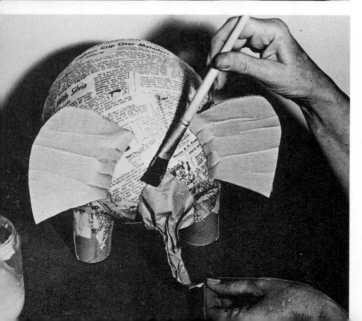

5. Aha! Our animal turns out to be an elephant. Ears cut from corrugated cardboard have been pasted in place. Now a piece of brown bag paper, crumpled and bent to form a trunk, is attached.

38

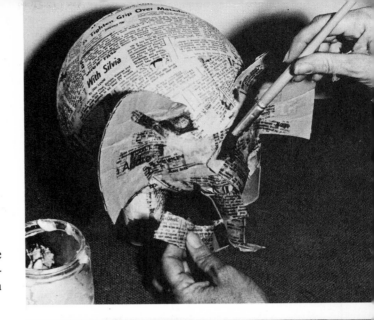

6. Completing the formation of the trunk by wrapping strips of damp newspaper around it and pasting them in place.

7. Applying mash. Here spoonfuls of mash are applied and troweled into place with a knife. (The surface was brushed with glue first.) This process will be continued until the entire surface is covered with a thin, even coating of mash. The spoon and the knife must be dipped into water from time to time and wiped clean with a sponge.

Where is the balloon? It is still inside the elephant. That is one advantage of using balloons—they are expendable. They can be left inside the shapes modeled over them and forgotten.

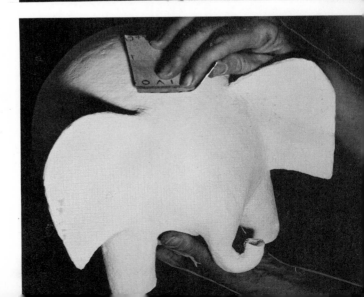

8. Sandpapering. When the mash has dried, it can be sandpapered if necessary. It is possible, however, to work a layer of mash onto a paper form in such a way that no sandpapering will be required. When the mash has dried, it will not have a smooth surface like that of chinaware, but will have a kind of orange-peel surface which, for some objects, is just right.

9. The elephant has been given one coat of white water-base acrylic paint.

The finished elephant is shown in color plate 7. The decoration was painted with poster colors and with gold lacquer. Four coats of clear lacquer were sprayed on when the colors were dry.

The elephant in the last photo series was made by pasting strips of paper around the balloon. Can mash be applied directly to a balloon without preliminary paper construction? Yes it can, but with a large balloon it is not easy. Large areas of wet mash are quite difficult to manage. If a smaller balloon is used, however, the mash can be applied directly to the surface. Let's try it.

PHOTO SERIES 9
A pair of Blooney birds

(What are Blooney birds? Birds made over balloons, naturally!)

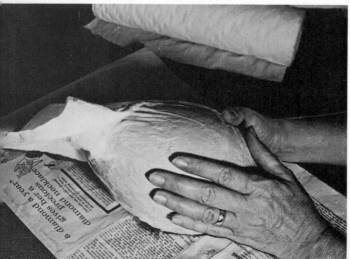

1. A handful of mash is patted onto the surface of a small pear-shaped balloon.

2. When the entire surface has been covered with an even coating of mash, slightly over ⅛ inch thick, the balloon is wrapped in paper towels as shown here. This blots up some of the excess moisture.

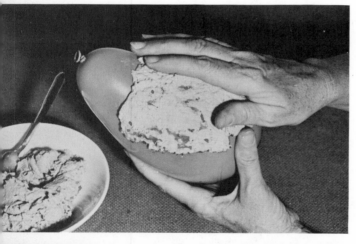

40

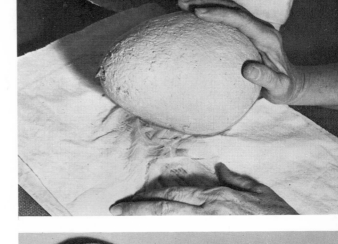

3. When the toweling is unwrapped, the pear-shaped shell is ready to put aside for drying. This is such a simple process—let's cover another balloon in the same manner.

4. What can we make out of two pear-shaped forms? Lots of things, for example a pair of birds, one long-legged, the other short. The body forms are in opposite positions: wide part on top in one, narrow part on top in the other. The legs here are made of coat hangers. The feet are temporary shapes of plastilene.

Beaks have been built up with paper and paste and mash. Beads of mash have been pressed on for eyes and a pipe cleaner is tried out as a crest.

5. Fastening the legs of the tall bird to the body. A portion of the shell has been cut out with a paring knife. The ends of the two long legs are fastened in place on the inside of the body with paste, paper and mash. When this is done, the cut out portion of the shell will be put back in place and the seam will be sealed with paper and paste.

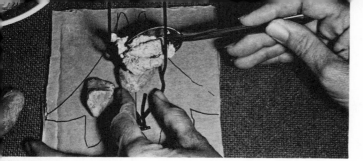

6. Feet for the tall bird. Because of his long legs, the feet must be large and heavily weighted to provide balance. Here the two feet are being formed together on a piece of cardboard with several pebbles inside.

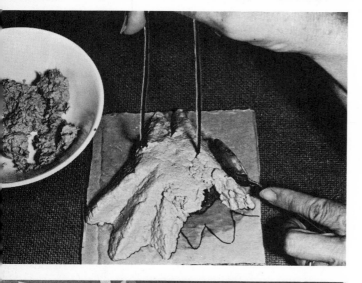

7. Finishing the feet. The legs and feet of the short bird were formed and fastened in place in the same manner as those of his long-legged companion.

8. The shaping of the two birds is completed.

9. The finished birds. Shorty was painted with enamels applied directly on the hardened mash. "High boy" was painted with tempera colors and sprayed with several coats of lacquer. The crests are made of laminated colored papers.

LAMINATION

If two or more pieces of paper are pasted together and then rolled or twisted into a shape while the paper is wet, the paper will hold the form when it dries. This is a type of construction useful in paper sculpture. We shall use this method to make jewelry in chapter 9.

6

PAPER

SCULPTURE

Wʜᴇɴ a commercial artist speaks of paper sculpture, he refers
to shapes made by cutting, scoring, rolling, folding and fastening
paper. Original and amusing objects are created this way; they appear
from time to time as displays in department store windows and in
advertising photographs. This is a sophisticated form of art and the
people who create in this medium have great talent, yet the things
they make are temporary, meant to be enjoyed for a brief period,
then discarded.

We are concerned with making more lasting things out of paper,
but let's say a word about temporary creations—party favors, Christmas
tree ornaments and the like. Plate 5 shows a figure to grace the

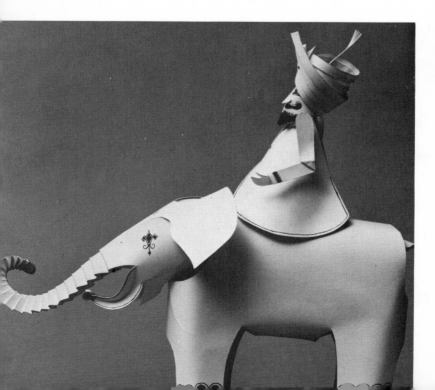

4. Elephant and
Rajah—paper sculp-
ture. (*Photograph by
Ben Gonzales, Jane
Lander Associates*)

44

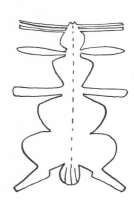

5. Easter bunny with
decorated egg

breakfast table on Easter morning, a bunny holding an Easter egg.
This little figure was made by cutting a pattern like the one shown
in the sketch, folding it as indicated and fastening with bits of cellophane tape at the neck, tummy and the ends of the forelegs.

The watch dog shown in plate 6 stood under the tree one Christmas morning with a watch around his neck—a present to a little girl.
Watch dog proved so well loved that he was not thrown away, but

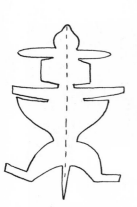

6. Watch dog

45

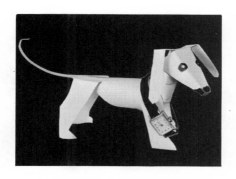

7. Lion made of mash, pressed on a cardboard cutout pattern

continues to stand each night on guard on the dresser, wearing his watch.

The lion in plate 7 is more solid. He, too, started out as a folded pattern as shown in plate 8. The pattern was folded, coated with glue to make it stronger, then bits of white mash were applied. The mane was made of crumpled wet kraft paper.

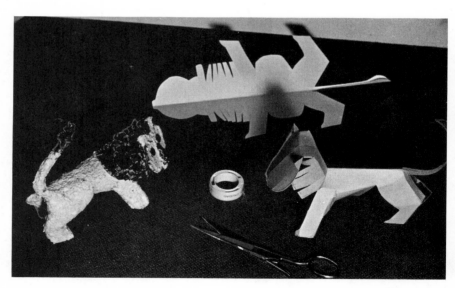

8. Steps in making the lion

But paper sculpture need not be temporary. Lasting objects can be modeled directly in paper and made strong and durable. There is almost no limit in subject matter or in size. Here are the steps in modeling a cat—starting with a paper bag.

PHOTO SERIES 10
Reclining cat

1. A paper bag has been stuffed with crumpled newspaper and tied into a shape resembling a fat sausage. Newspaper strips are being pasted around the bag. Tear a piece of newspaper three inches wide, brush paste on it, then fold over one side half-way to the center, brush with paste again and fold the other side over. This produces a strip of pasted paper three layers thick and about one inch wide. Such strips can be wound like bandages around a stuffed paper bag to build up form.

2. More strips have been wrapped around and pasted in place.

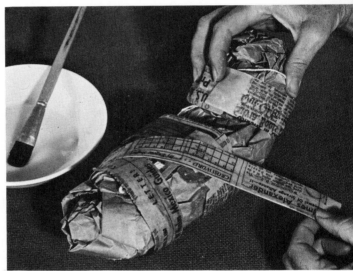

3. A layer of brown kraft paper has been pasted over the entire body. The head has been shaped roughly and the beginnings of ears have been formed. Tubes have been rolled out of damp kraft paper to form legs and tail. Pieces of kraft paper soaking in the bowl of paste will be used for modeling details.

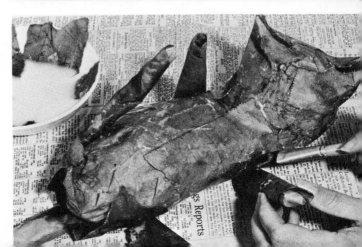

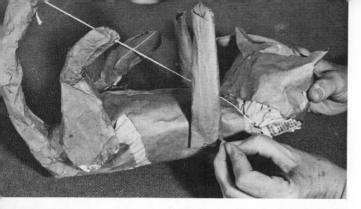

4. More shape has been given to the legs and the tail. Here the left foreleg is being pinned in place on the body. The tail is held in position by a piece of string.

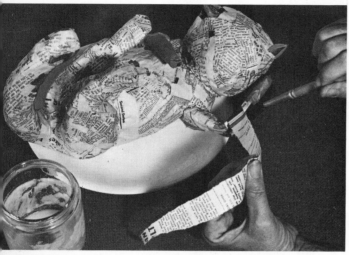

5. Modeling is carried further with strips of damp paper and paste. The figure is resting in a soup plate. This serves as a practical type of modeling stand. The work is held in position and can be rotated easily.

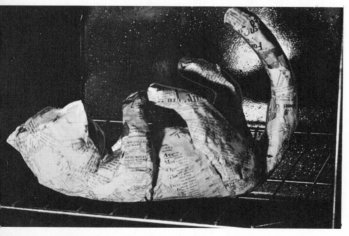

6. In the oven for drying.

7. The paper sculpture has been completely covered with a layer of mash (the form was brushed with diluted glue before mash was applied). The mash has dried. Now the surface is being finished by sandpapering. Features have been tentatively sketched in.

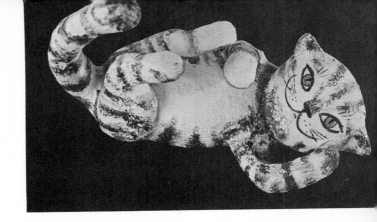

8. The finished cat.

A piece of sculpture in paper does not have to begin with a paper bag. A framework on which to paste paper can be constructed out of corrugated cardboard as shown in the following series:

PHOTO SERIES 11
A stylized head

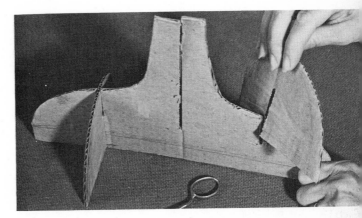

1. A framework for the neck and shoulders is constructed of corrugated cardboard.

2. Strips of paper, like those used in making the cat, have been wrapped around the vertical portion to form a neck. More strips to form shoulders and bustline are held in place by paper clips. A balloon covered with newspaper and paste is held in place and tried for size.

49

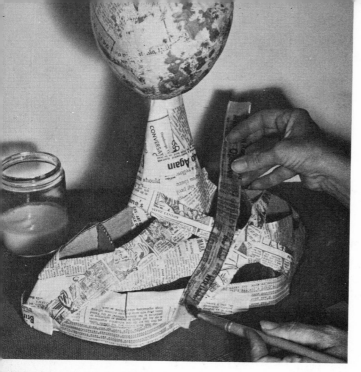

3. The head has been pasted in place (it was smoothed with sandpaper). Strips of paper are used to build up the shoulders and bust. Plenty of paste is used.

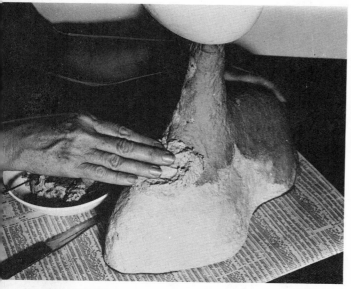

4. After newspaper construction has been completed and allowed to dry, the final surface is built up by applying paper mash. This is patted into place with the fingertips. When it dries, the mash can be sanded smooth.

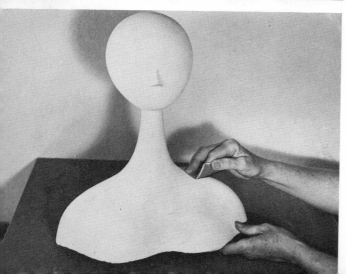

5. Finishing. A nose of mash was added. After the entire surface had been sanded smooth, the sculpture was given a base coat of gesso. Here, after the base coat has dried, the sculpture is given a final sandpapering; when this is done, it will be sprayed with three coats of mat finish lacquer.

What!—no hair, no eyes, no painted decoration? No, not on this piece. We have here an exercise in pure form.

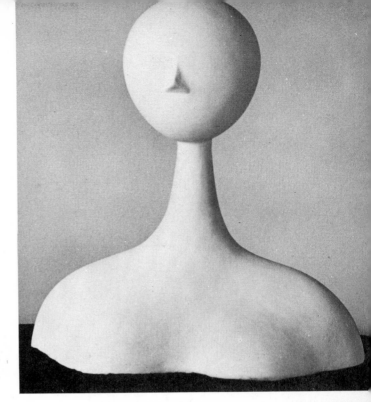

6, 7 and 8. The finished bust. Changing directions of sunlight create constant changing patterns of light and shade. (*Photographs by Roy Rosen*)

51

9. Scene in a piñata shop

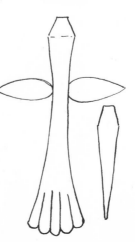

The next photo series illustrates two different ways of modeling a lion in paper.

PHOTO SERIES 12
Lions

1. The shape of a lion is built up with strips of newspaper soaked in liquid starch. A cardboard core from a roll of toilet paper was used as the initial support for the form. No brush is used—modeling is done with the fingers.

2. Modeling of the body is completed with mash. The mane is made of strips of newspaper soaked in starch, the tail is a pipe cleaner dipped in starch then covered with strips of paper napkin.

When the mash dried, the body of the figure was painted with white water-base wall paint to which red dry pigment had been added. The mane was brushed with pink and, when dry, the edges of the mane were touched with gold lacquer. The finished lion is shown in color plate 22.

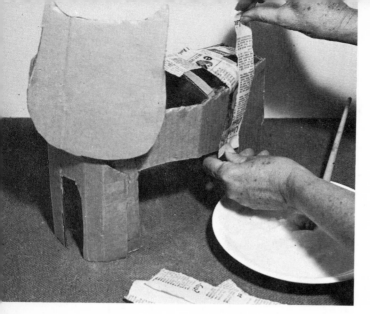

3. Another lion. A cardboard framework is covered with strips of newspaper soaked in thin paste. Most of the modeling is done with the fingers.

4. The finished lion. The body was painted with blue enamel, orange enamel was used on the face, and the mane was painted gold. Flower shapes cut from colored paper were pasted on the body and outlined with white paint. (Who says all lions look alike?)

54

The next series shows another kind of paper sculpture—making and draping a figurine.

PHOTO SERIES 13
A singer

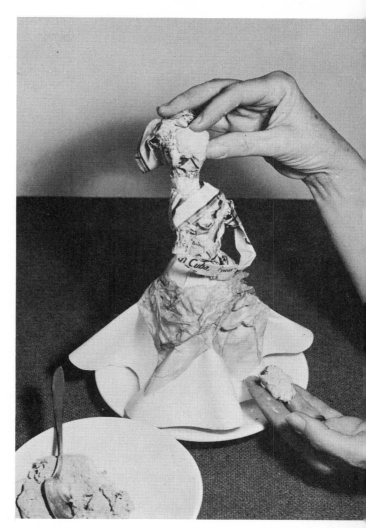

1. A figurine 10 inches tall is built up over a portion of the core from a roll of paper towels. The body has been roughly shaped of newspaper soaked in diluted glue. The face is being modeled in mash.

The skirt is made of a circle cut from white drawing paper, soaked in diluted glue. Tissue paper, also soaked in thin glue, forms an overskirt.

2. Modeling of the figure has been carried further. Mash has been used to form features, arms, bust and coiffure.

A strip of paper lace, cut from a paper doily, is used to trim the edge of the skirt.

55

3. The finished work.

DRAPING

A costume on a figurine can be created by draping with pieces of old cotton sheeting. The cloth is soaked in paste or diluted glue. The adhesive is worked into the cloth with the fingers, then the excess is squeezed out. The saturated cloth is fastened to the figurine while the figurine and the cloth are still wet. Embroidered and lace edgings may also be draped and adhered in this fashion. Artists who work in this medium are able to create elaborate costumes.

Sculpture in paper can be made in many different ways. We have explored some of these, but there are others.

One method, especially good for making masks, uses plastilene. The face is modeled in plastilene. Then a shell is formed by pasting layers of paper over the model. When the paper dries, the mask is

56

lifted off. This method can also be used for small figures in the round as we shall see in photo series 24 in chapter 10.

There are so many approaches to sculpture. Creations may be playful or austere, realistic or stylized, classical in feeling or ultra-modern. Paper and mash lend themselves to almost any kind of expression. As you work with this medium and acquire skill, you will find the methods that suit you best and will develop your own individual style.

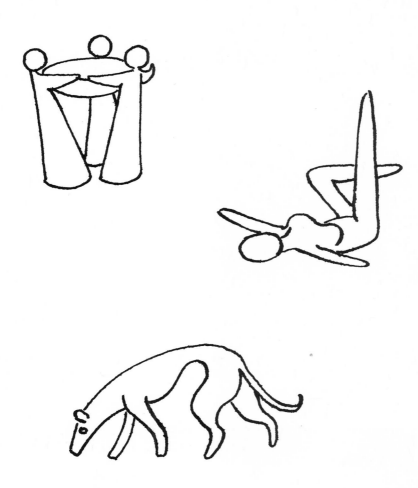

7

PRESSING

IN

MOLDS

In chapter 4 we made shapes by pressing mash on the outside surfaces of bowls. If, instead, we were to press mash on the inside surface of a dish, we would obtain a truer shape with a smoother surface. Here are the steps in making a piece of paper sculpture by using a soup plate as a mold.

PHOTO SERIES 14
Pressing a disk

1. A soup plate was given a coating of petroleum jelly. Then the excess jelly was wiped out with a paper towel, leaving a thin, even coating on the plate. Here paper pulp is pressed into the plate. This is paper pulp with nothing added. Mash mixed according to the recipe in chapter 2 would be apt to stick to the bowl even though a liberal coating of petroleum jelly were used. The spoon is used to press the pulp into a tight, compact layer ¼ inch thick. Excess moisture can be blotted from the pulp with paper towels.

After the layer is formed, the bowl is turned upside down for drying. The work may be left overnight standing on several layers of newspaper, or drying may be hastened by putting the bowl upside down in a warm oven, on three or four sheets of newspaper.

2. After the layer of pulp has dried, the pressing lifts out easily. Since the material contains no glue, it is soft and can be easily torn. But a coat of glue brushed over the surface at this point adds a great deal of strength.

What can we do with the disk we have made? How about making a wall plaque with a sun face design?

3. A geometrical pattern of sun rays has been cut from a piece of corrugated cardboard. Smaller triangular shapes have been cut out to serve as intermediate rays.

4. The edges of the corrugated cardboard have been sealed with damp newspaper and paste. The disk has been pasted in place and so have the shorter rays.

59

5. The completed plaque. The work was given a coat of gesso. Then three coats of diluted glue (one part glue, one part water) were brushed on with time allowed for each coat to dry. After that, the features were painted with casein colors and the outer rays were painted with bronze powder (brilliant gold) mixed with clear varnish. When the paint was dry, two more coats of diluted glue were brushed over all areas except the gold rays. When the last coat of glue was dry, a coat of clear varnish was brushed on.

PHOTO SERIES 15
Another plaque

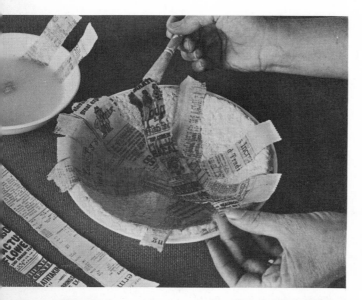

1. A different kind of sun face made by a slightly different method. Pulp has been pressed into a soup plate (coated with petroleum jelly first). Now strips of newspaper are being pasted onto the back of the pulp to give strength and to help in the construction which is to follow.

2. Rays are made by rolling cones of newspaper and paste, then squeezing them to resemble tongues of flame.

60

3. The flaming rays, irregular in size and shape, have been pasted around the rim of the disk. The ends of the newspaper strips that were pasted on the back help in fastening the rays. Features are sketched with a felt marker.

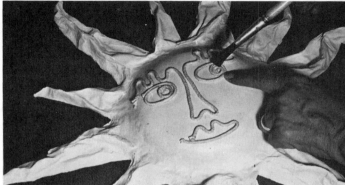

4. When the rays were completed and dry, the work was given a coat of gesso. Features are outlined in medium heavy twine dipped in glue and fastened in place. After this step was completed, the plaque was painted with powdered brilliant bronze mixed with clear lacquer.

5. The finished plaque. An antique effect was achieved by brushing on walnut varnish thinned with turpentine. Paper toweling was used to wipe off the excess varnish immediately, leaving the dark tones in the crevices of the design.

The two plaques made in this chapter have similar motifs, yet they are quite different in appearance. The first one has a high-gloss finish and a type of formal symmetry. The surface obtained by brushing glue and then varnish over smooth gesso resembles that of porcelain.

The second plaque is less symmetrical with a surface that is rougher in texture. The use of crumpled newspaper for the rays and cord for the features gives an additional dimension to the design. These two pieces illustrate the great versatility of papier mâché and the opportunities it offers to those interested in exploring its possibilities.

8

PLASTER

OF

PARIS

A soup plate is satisfactory as a mold if we want to press a papier mâché disk. For a more complicated shape, we must make our own mold out of plaster of Paris. Plaster of Paris (calcined gypsum) is a fine white powder which, when mixed with water and allowed to stand, sets into a hard, white mass. It can be bought in one- or two-pound packages in hardware stores or art supply shops. There are many different kinds. The best for mold making is pottery plaster, the type used in ceramic work. If this is not easily obtainable, buy the best grade of molding plaster available. Plaster does not stay fresh a long time after the package is opened, so buy a small quantity at a time.

To make a mold, we must first prepare a model using clay or plastilene. Plastilene, a prepared modeling material made of clay ground with oil, does not harden and can be used over and over. It is better than regular clay for the papier mâché craftsman. It can be bought from art supply dealers.

The model must be a simple shape without any undercuts, that is, the widest part must be at the base, and there must be no indentation at the sides in which the mold would grip the model and hold it fast. Here are the steps in making a model and casting a mold.

PHOTO SERIES 16
A one-piece press mold

1. Two fish shapes are modeled in plastilene. A large dinner plate serves as a work table. Modeling tools are the handle of a spoon and a paring knife.

2. Two smaller fish shapes have been modeled. These can be used to make a pair of earrings; the larger fish can be used for earrings or pins.

The dinner plate was coated with petroleum jelly and then wiped clean with a paper napkin before the fish were put in position. A retaining wall 1½ inches high, to hold the plaster of Paris, is made of plastilene. The fish and the retaining wall have been pressed firmly against the plate so that, when plaster is poured, it will not seep under the plastilene.

MIXING PLASTER

Ceramic artists, when they make molds, measure the proportions of plaster and water carefully, using 2¾ pounds of plaster to one

63

quart of water. If there is no scale at hand for weighing the plaster, the quantity can be estimated.

A mold for our fish will require a pint of water. Put the water into a clean container (a plastic bowl is best), and sprinkle plaster into the water slowly until the plaster forms a small mound above the surface of the water. Let the plaster slake (that is, soak up water) for two minutes. By that time the mound of plaster will have sunk into the water. Then stir.

Stirring should be done with a large spoon. Agitate the whole mass evenly and stir from the bottom upward in order to get rid of air bubbles. Don't whip the mixture—that puts more air bubbles in. Stirring should continue for two or three minutes. When the mixture starts to thicken it is time to pour.

POURING PLASTER

Plaster must be poured smoothly without splashing. Pour a small quantity on the model first and then blow gently so that every portion of the model is covered with plaster. This will avoid the danger of having air bubbles or vacant spaces next to the model. Then continue to pour plaster until the entire space within the retaining wall is filled.

3. Pouring plaster.

After the plaster has been poured, the table should be jarred in order to force any remaining air bubbles to the surface. The plaster must be left undisturbed while it sets. In a short time the surface of the plaster will lose its shine; after that it will start to harden and become warm. After several more minutes have elapsed, it will start to cool. When it is quite cold to the touch, the setting action is completed.

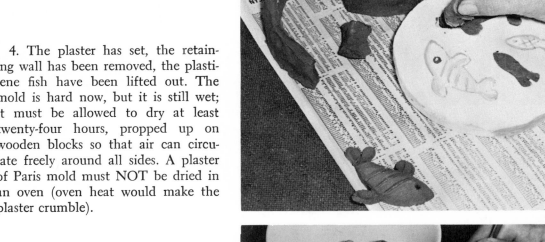

4. The plaster has set, the retaining wall has been removed, the plastilene fish have been lifted out. The mold is hard now, but it is still wet; it must be allowed to dry at least twenty-four hours, propped up on wooden blocks so that air can circulate freely around all sides. A plaster of Paris mold must NOT be dried in an oven (oven heat would make the plaster crumble).

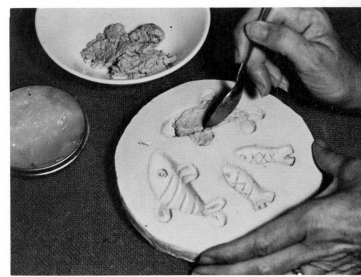

5. Pressing. After the mold was thoroughly dry, a thin coating of petroleum jelly was brushed into the depressions, then all of the jelly was wiped out with a paper napkin. Wet paper pulp (pulp alone with no glue added) is pressed into the mold. Tiny loops of thin wire were put into the pulp at the nose of each fish to serve as hangers when the fish are converted into earrings.

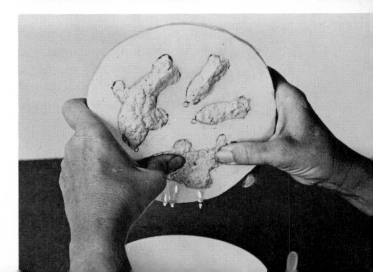

6. Pressing must be done firmly so that pulp fills every portion of the mold and so that as much water as possible is squeezed out of the pulp. The mold should be held upside down over a bowl while the pulp is pressed with the thumbs so that excess water can run off. When the pressing is completed, the pulp should be blotted with a paper towel.

7. After the pressings are thoroughly dry, the fish can be easily lifted out of the mold. Rough edges can be trimmed with a knife or a pair of scissors. (Pressed paper pulp is too soft to sandpaper.)

8. The fish are given a coat of white glue. This adds strength and makes the surface suitable for painting.

CLEANING UP

Disposal of plaster waste can present a problem. A bowl in which plaster has been mixed must not be rinsed in the kitchen sink—there is danger of clogging the drain. If a plastic bowl is used, the plaster can be left in the bowl until it sets hard, then when the bowl is squeezed the plaster will crack out. If a glass or pottery bowl is used, it can either be wiped with newspaper before the plaster sets or, if the plaster has set hard in the bowl, cold water may be poured in. This will cause the plaster to break away from the bowl so that it can be disposed of as ordinary waste.

We have made a mold and pressed some small fish shapes. Later on we shall see how molds can be used for larger papier mâché projects. Meanwhile, in chapter 9 we shall convert the fish into earrings and learn how to make other kinds of papier mâché jewelry.

9

JEWELRY

COLORFUL and original costume jewelry can be made of papier mâché at almost no cost. One can be completely free in creating designs for such jewelry since there is no fear of wasting precious metals or gems.

Color plate 10 shows several pairs of earrings and some brooches made of the fish pressed in the mold that was made in chapter 8. (Findings—ear clips and pins—can be bought in hobby supply shops.) Beads and bits of glass jewelry have been glued on for eyes. Beads have also been attached to some of the metal ear clips. The ear clips on the pair of small gold fish have gold mounds that were made of bread paste and then painted with gold lacquer (bronze powder and clear lacquer).

BREAD PASTE

This material is useful in making papier mâché jewelry. It is a strong adhesive that can be used to make settings for jewels on rings or bracelets or earrings. It dries hard with a fine surface to paint on.

Bread paste is made of fresh white bread, glue, glycerine and water. The inside portion of two slices of bread (no crust) is crumbled and kneaded. Dip the fingers into water occasionally to moisten the thick, doughy paste slightly. Roll it into a ball, push the thumb into the center to make a little depression; in this put four drops of glue and one drop of glycerine. Knead the glue and glycerine into the mass. When the dough is smooth and free from lumps, it is ready to use for jewelry settings. A very small lump of bread paste is sufficient to fasten a jewel to a papier mâché ring. When attaching such a jewel, a drop of glue should be put on the surface of the ring and on the bottom of the jewel. The jewel must be pressed firmly into the doughy ball.

This is a tricky, sticky material to work with, but if the fingers and the tools are rinsed frequently, bread paste can be used as a material to model small shapes, beads and tiny floral forms, as we shall see later in this chapter.

Earrings of a different type are shown in the making in plate 10. Patterns cut from light cardboard are folded to form tiny triangular pyramids, open at the bottom, then covered with paper and paste. After that a thin wire is glued into the apex of each pyramid and the work is brushed with a coating of glue. At the right, one of the pyramids dries, standing upside down in the air, its wire stuck into a wad of plastilene.

After the glue dried, small triangles of mirror (cut with a glass cutter from a scrap of mirror) were glued to each face of the pyra-

10. Making earrings

11. Rolling spirals of
laminated gold paper
for earrings

mids and light twine was fastened at the edges of the mirror. Then
all parts of the work except the mirror areas were given another coat
of glue and painted with tempera color and gold lacquer. Several
coats of clear lacquer were brushed on when the paint was dry.

The ear clips were decorated to match the pendants. A smaller
triangle of mirror was fastened to each clip with bread paste and
trimmed with light twine. A bit of paper lace was fastened at the
top of each clip, then the work was given a coat of glue and painted
with the same colors used in the pendants. Color plate 12 shows the
finished earrings.

LAMINATION

In plate 11 we see a pair of earrings being made by lamination.
Strips were cut from gold paper and from white drawing paper and
then pasted together so that three strips of white paper were in the
center and strips of gold paper (gold side out) on top and bottom.
When the pasting was done, the edges of the pasted strips were carefully trimmed. Then, before the paste had a chance to dry, the strips
were wrapped spiral fashion around the tapering handle of a paint
brush. (Note: The two spirals were twisted in opposite directions.)
Metal ear clips are shown in the center.

Color plate 11 shows the finished earrings. A bit of gold wire holds
the spirals to the ear clips which have been decorated with a coil
of twine pressed into bread paste, then painted with gold lacquer. As
a final touch, a pearl bead was glued in the center of the coil of twine.

69

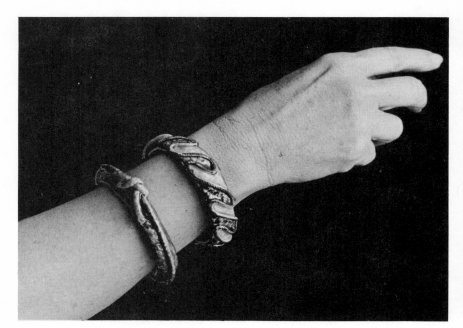

12. Bracelets decorated with cord

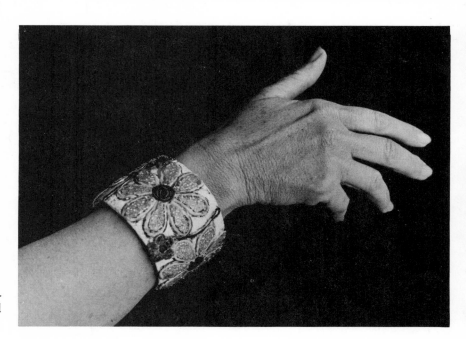

13. Bracelet decorated with twine and tiny glass beads

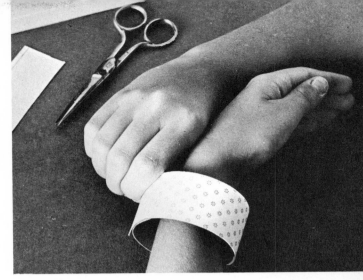

1. A 1½ inch wide strip of light cardboard from a facial tissue box is tried around the wrist for size. Then it is pasted.

2. Pieces of newspaper are pasted on the cardboard (inside as well as outside).

3. Several layers of newspaper have been pasted on the bracelet; now it has been put on a glass tumbler to make sure it remains circular. The tumbler was wrapped with newspaper first to keep the bracelet from sticking fast. A paring knife is used to press the paper into a smooth convex surface.

71

4. The bracelet remains on the tumbler while mash is pressed on. (Paste was brushed on first.)

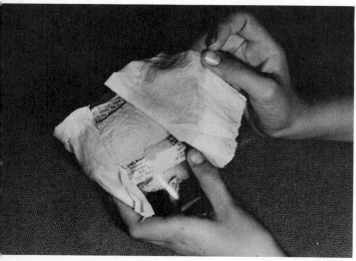

5. After all the mash has been applied, excess moisture is blotted off with a paper towel.

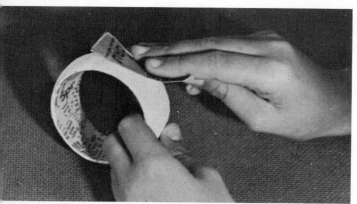

6. Sandpapering after the mash has dried thoroughly.

7. Decorating. Designs were lightly sketched on the bracelet. Colorful plastic beads and bits of mirror were fastened on with small mounds of bread paste. When the bread paste had set hard, twine was glued on to outline the shapes sketched. Poster colors and gold lacquer were brushed on to complete the design. Several coats of clear lacquer were sprayed on.

14. Uncoiling a cardboard core to make a bracelet

The core of a roll of toilet paper can be used for the beginning of a bracelet. These cores are made of spirals of cardboard. Plate 14 shows such a spiral unwrapped. Plate 15 shows the ends held together to make a shape on which a bracelet can be built up of paper, paste and mash. Color plate 13 shows the finished bracelet. Decorative details were added of cord and glass jewels strung on wire. (The wire was bent and imbedded in mash.) The bracelet was finished with gold lacquer after a coating of glue had dried.

15. Forming the bracelet

16. Beginning a ring

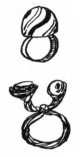

RINGS

Rings are simple to make. The first step may be pasting a strip of cardboard around the finger as shown in plate 16. Another way to begin, shown in plate 17, is to twist half a facial tissue into a tight rope, dip the rope in glue, wrap it around a finger for size, then slip the ring shape off and allow it to dry.

All sorts of things can be mounted on papier mâché rings—glass jewels, bits of mirror, designs made of bread paste and string, beads, marbles, abstract shapes modeled in mash, bread paste flowers.

BREAD PASTE FLOWERS

Tiny floral motifs for papier mâché jewelry can be made from bread paste as shown in plate 18. Prepare a ball of dough as described earlier in this chapter; roll a number of small balls, add a bit of casein color or powdered pigment to each ball, then knead in the color thoroughly. Add a little plain bread paste if the color seems too strong. Tear off a piece of colored dough the size of a pea, roll it, flatten it between the thumb and forefinger until it is quite thin, then shape it into a petal. Twist one end onto a thin wire or a toothpick. Make another petal, place it in similar position next to the first petal and continue adding petals, curling them outward and unfolding as you go. (It is good to have some real flowers at hand as models.) Petals can be cut to make flowers resembling asters, chrysanthemums,

74

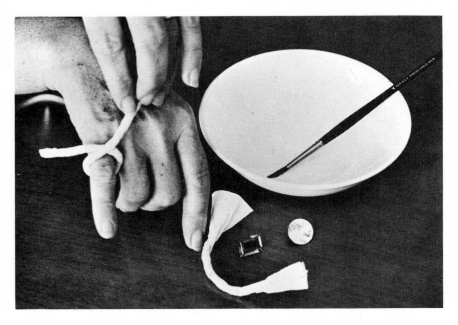

17. Another way to make a ring

daisies, etc. Leaves may be cut from flattened pieces also. The wire should be covered with green floral tape before leaves are added. When bread paste flowers are dry, they should be brushed with clear lacquer. This gives them a surface resembling that of porcelain.

18. Making bread paste flowers

75

19. Flower plaque by Sra. L. Valera Gomez

Plate 19 shows a framed bouquet 6½ inches tall. The flowers and leaves are bread paste. The berries were made by pressing bread paste through a piece of nylon net. The ball of paste was not detached from the net but the excess net was trimmed off, leaving enough so that the berry could be attached to a stem. The dried grass in the bouquet is real; it has been brushed with gold lacquer.

10
INTERIOR
DECOR

Papier mâché has much to offer the home planner who wishes to make special, original, unique pieces for the household. Picture frames, candleholders, wall brackets, cocktail tables and other paper creations are decorative and functional.

The following project shows how a discarded scrap of mirror, an irregular rectangle with damaged edges and a hole in one corner, was salvaged. By planning an oval frame, it was possible to use the mirror without the rough edges or the hole being seen.

An oval (ellipse) can be drawn with two thumbtacks, a piece of string tied into a loop, and a pencil, as shown in the sketch.

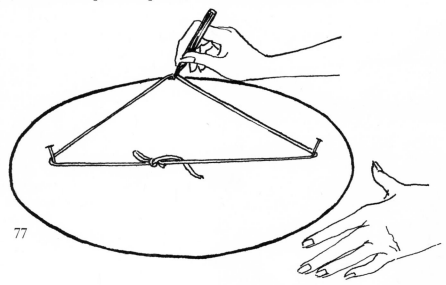

77

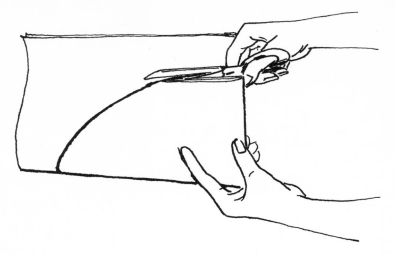

Another way to make an elliptical or oval shape is to fold a sheet of newspaper in half, then in quarters. With a pair of scissors, cut one quarter of an elliptical curve, then unfold the paper and study the shape. If it is not right, fold the paper once more and trim the curve. Repeating this process several times (using more newspaper if necessary), will produce a satisfactory oval pattern.

PHOTO SERIES 18
An oval mirror frame

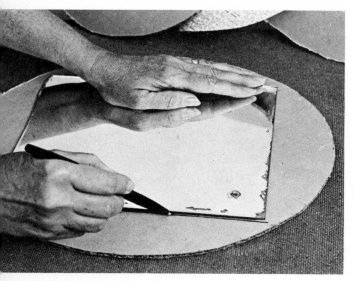

1. An elliptical shape slightly larger than the mirror has been cut from corrugated cardboard. The mirror is placed on the cardboard oval and the outline is traced. The space within this outline will be cut out. In the background are two more ovals similar to the one in the foreground. One of them has an elliptical opening cut in it; this will be the face of the frame. The other has no opening. It will be the back.

2. The edge of the inner curve of the frame's face is being bound with newspaper and paste to conceal the rough edge of the corrugated cardboard. The mirror is shown in place in the cardboard oval from which a rectangle was cut to receive it.

3. The three pieces of cardboard are being bound together. The portion with the opening, the face of the frame, is on top. Under it is the piece of cardboard containing the mirror, and under that is the oval which forms the back of the frame. These three cardboard ovals with the mirror in place have been glued together. While the mirror frame rests on a glass jar, a paper binding is pasted around the edge.

4. Rolling the edge to make it smooth. The edge has been bound with a layer of newspaper and a second layer of brown kraft paper. While the binding is still wet, the frame is rolled on the table top to make the edge true and even.

5. A hanger. The mirror in its frame lies face down while a piece of twine is pasted to the back with strips of kraft paper. Note that the back has been covered with newspaper.

79

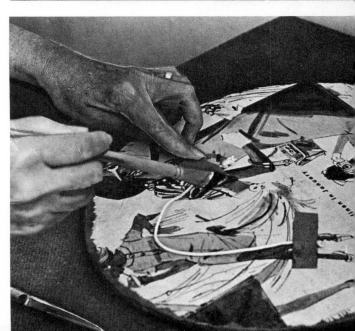

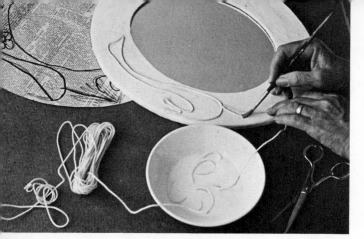

6. Decorating with twine. A design of birds and flowers sketched on a newspaper oval is being duplicated on the mirror frame with twine and glue.

7. The completed mirror. This was painted with enamels, stippled with gold lacquer and sprayed with clear plastic lacquer.

The small mirror we just made is a simple one. It looks like what it is: something made of paper, decorated with string and paint. Yet it is gay and amusing, well suited to hang in a child's room.

1. Boxes

2. Box with hinged lid, covered with gift wrapping paper

3. Cylindrical boxes, covered with gift wrapping papers and a bark painting

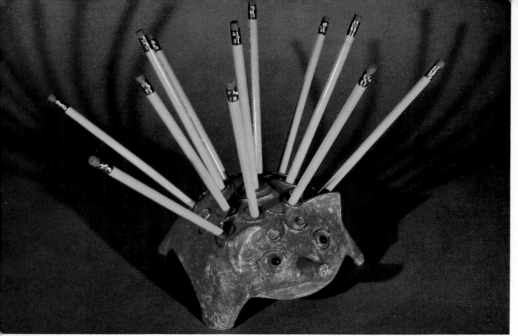

4. Porky Pencilpine

5. Owl (collection of Mr. and Mrs. Stanley Cohen, Washington, D. C.)

6. Another Porky, a different color scheme (collection of Sra. Ramon Prats, Cuernavaca, Mexico)

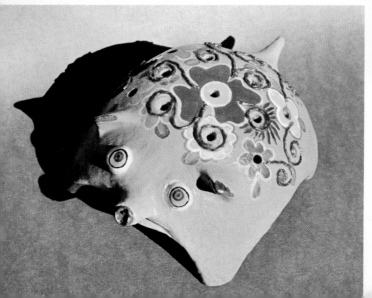

7. Elephant

8. Blooney birds

9. Wall plaque (collection of
Mr. and Mrs. Pat Thompson,
Moultrie, Ga.)

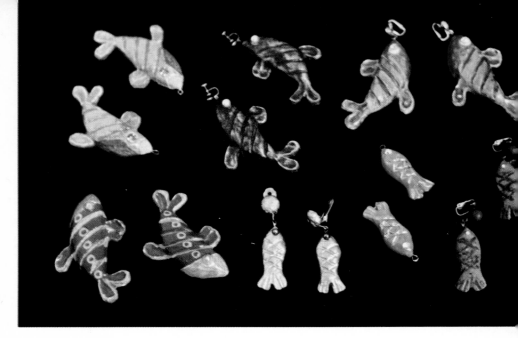

10. Fish pressed in molds, for use in earrings or brooches

11. and 12. Papier mâché jewelry

13. Bracelet

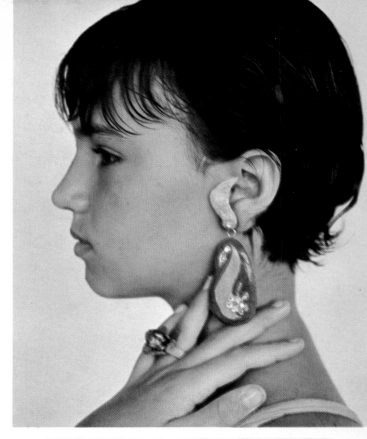

14. Papier mâché jewelry

15. Blue lion

16. Bread paste flowers by
Lala V. de Valera

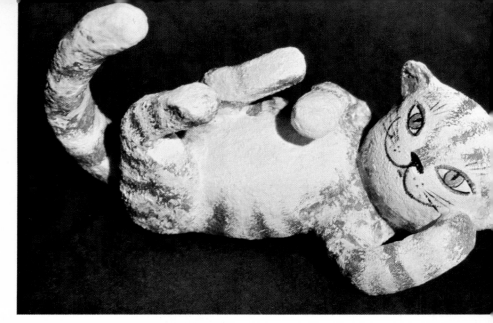

17. Pussy cat (collection of Capt. and Mrs. Hampton Hubbard, Bethesda, Md.)

18. Tony

19. Straw dispensing bird

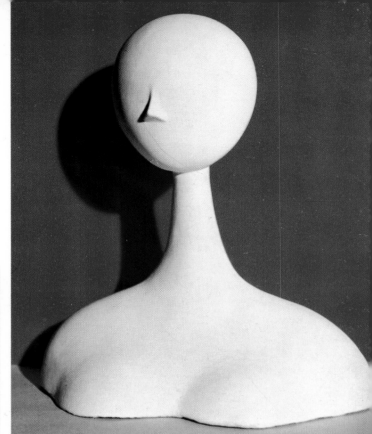

20. Stylized bust

21. Figurine, a singer

22. Red lion

23. Baroque mirror

24. Mirror for
a child's room

25. Wall bracket

26. Wall plaque (collection of Lini M.
de Vries, Educational Dir., Institute for
Mexican Studies)

28. Birthday bird

27. Flower girl (paper flowers shown here but she can hold real flowers, too)

30. Monsieur le Duc

29. Three-armed candleholder

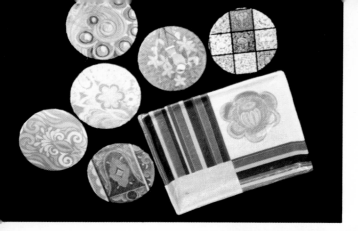

31. Snack tray and coasters, covered with gift wrapping papers

32. Tray, montage design

33. Tray with Indian painting mounted on

34. Lamp, papier mâché built over
two tin cans

35. Rectangular lamp, papier mâché
built over three tin cans

36. Lamp for a child's room

37. The lamp
lighted

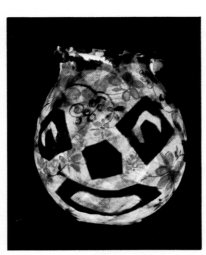

38. Translucent globe, fern montage

39. Cocktail table

40. Translucent globe, montage of colored cellophane; pedestal covered with gift wrapping paper

41. Maud, a mermaid, eight feet,
four inches long, from head to tail

42. Wall plaque (collection of Frances P. Mellen, Publisher, Mexico City, Mexico)

43. Stage prop for *Waltz of the Toreadors*

44. Miriam (collection of Edee Greene, Woman's Editor, *Fort Lauderdale News*, Florida)

45. Garden girl . . . Wearing her black wig and a pink paper bikini

46. and 47. Wearing her blonde wig and a bikini made of gift wrapping papers

48. Pair of wall plaques, rooster and hen; rooster is 30 inches tall; hen decorated with montage of gift wrapping papers

49. Helga, abstract garden sculpture; fifty-four inches tall (collection of Col. and Mrs. N. Anthony Armstrong, Cuernavaca, Mexico)

Our next project is a different kind of papier mâché frame, larger, with a baroque design that makes it appropriate for more formal interiors. The mirror is 18 inches wide by 24 inches high, with a triangle 6 inches wide by 9 inches high cut from each corner. (A mirror can be cut at home with a glass cutter, or the store where you buy the mirror will cut it.) Three large pieces of corrugated cardboard form the frame: one with an elliptical opening for the face, one with the opening cut to hold the mirror, and one with no opening, to form the back. The outer edges of the three pieces of cardboard are cut to identical shape, an oval with projections at the sides and ends to hold ornaments.

The design on the face of the frame is built up with paper and paste, then covered with mash. When the mash has dried, it is brushed with glue and given a coat of spackle.

SPACKLE

This is patching plaster, sold in hardware stores under such names as "spackling putty," "plastic patch," etc. It is a slow-setting type of plaster of Paris which, when mixed with water to form a thick paste, can be modeled into various shapes. If more water is used so that the mixture has the consistency of thick cream, it can be brushed over paper constructions that have been coated with glue. After two or three hours, when spackle sets, it is easily carved or sandpapered.

PHOTO SERIES 19
A baroque mirror frame

1. The mirror rests on a large piece of cardboard while its outline is traced. The space within this outline will be cut out to hold the mirror. An elliptical pattern for the opening of the frame has been cut from newspaper.

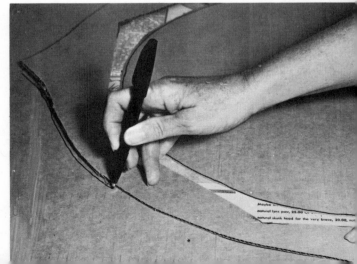

2. The outer edge of the piece of cardboard with the opening for the mirror has been cut into an oval shape with projections at the sides and ends. This is being traced on another piece of cardboard in which an elliptical opening, the size of the paper pattern, has been cut. The edge of the elliptical opening has been bound with newspaper and paste. When the lower piece of cardboard has been trimmed on the traced outline, it will form the base for the face of the frame. A third piece of cardboard trimmed to the same shape (with no opening) will be the back.

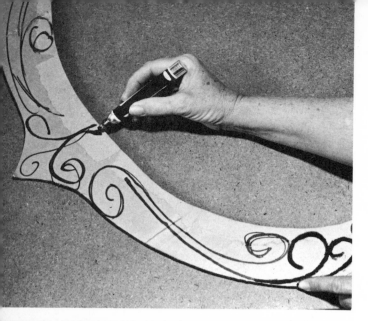

3. A rococo design is sketched on the face of the frame. A second binding of kraft paper has been pasted on the inner edge.

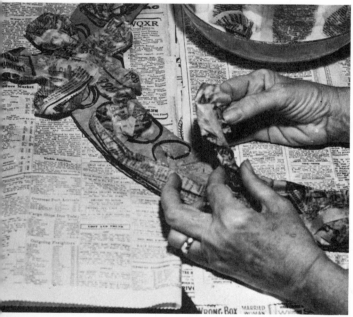

4. The design is built up with pieces of newspaper soaked in paste.

5. Mash is put on top of the newspaper.

6. Modeling is done with mash. (A spoon is a good modeling tool.)

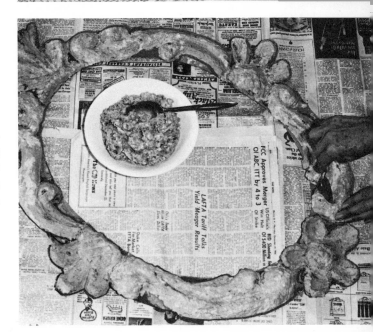

7. Modeling in mash is carried further. At this point it was decided that the floral motif shown in the lower right corner was not in keeping with the rest of the design, so it was cut out.

8. A shell motif to replace the flower is modeled of paper and mash. A plastic turntable is used.

9. When the mash dried, the three pieces of cardboard forming the frame were glued together with the mirror in place, protected by a sheet of newspaper. After that, spackle mixed with water was brushed over the entire design. When the spackle dried, finishing touches were given with sandpaper and paring knife.

10. Painting. Two coats of bronze powder (brilliant gold) mixed with clear lacquer were brushed on. When the painting was dry, the protective layer of newspaper was carefully cut out with a razor blade.

11. The completed frame.

A wall bracket is an attractive and useful accessory, easy to construct.

PHOTO SERIES 20
A wall bracket

1. The platform of the bracket planned here will be a semi-circle, ten inches in diameter, held up by three rococo supports. The semi-circle with a tongue for a vertical support has been cut from a cardboard box. This piece was cut from the box in such a way that a corner of the box made the angle between the platform and the vertical support. A hole has been punched in the center at the top of the support. This will be used to hang the bracket. A second semi-circle without a vertical support has been cut out. For proper thickness, three layers of corrugated cardboard are needed. Scraps of corrugated cardboard are pasted on the second semi-circle.

2. The two semi-circles have been fastened together with the cardboard scraps in between. The edge of the bracket shelf is being sealed with pieces of wet newspaper and paste.

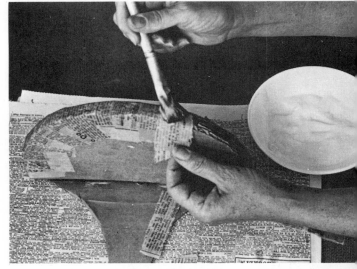

3. Placing the supports. Three curved pieces have been cut from corrugated cardboard. These are being fastened into place with strips of wet newspaper and paste.

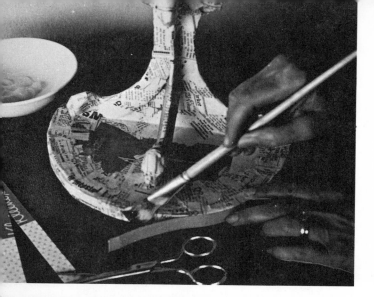

4. A strip of light cardboard is pasted on the edge of the shelf. This will give a smooth outer edge on which cord will be pasted later. Bits of wet newspaper and paste have been pressed over the ends of the supports to form ball shapes.

5. Mash is pressed onto the supports and molded into shape.

6. After modeling is completed and the mash has dried, a coating of spackle is brushed over the entire surface of the bracket.

86

7. Three pieces of heavy cord are glued to the edge of the shelf.

8. The completed bracket. This was given two coats of bronze powder (brilliant gold) mixed with clear lacquer.

The next series shows the construction of another type of bracket, one made to fit on the arm of a chair. The chair is a comfortable lounge type, but the arms slope at such an angle that glasses or ash trays placed there slide off. A papier mâché bracket tailored to fit on the arm provides a level surface for holding a cup of coffee.

PHOTO SERIES 21
A chair arm bracket

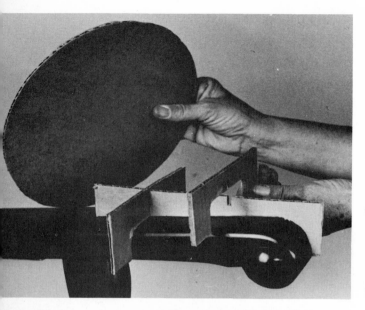

1. Three pieces of corrugated cardboard have been cut so that they will fit together, forming a framework that grips the arm of the chair. When the framework is in place, its top is horizontal. A circle cut from corrugated cardboard will form a platform on top of the framework.

2. Applying mash. The chair arm is protected by a sheet of thin plastic while mash is built up around the framework.

After this the cardboard disk was given a coating of glue and covered on both sides with mash. It was dried in an oven under weights so that it would not warp, then it was glued to the construction that had been built up on the chair arm.

3. The bracket in use. It is not painted; the mash, made of newspaper and some business correspondence (envelopes with stamps, etc.), dried with an attractive surface flecked with bits of color. (A piece of gold wrapping paper was used in the mash also.) Several coats of spray-on lacquer made the bracket easy to clean with a damp sponge.

Candlesticks—ah, these are really fun to make. They can be designed in so many different ways—made simple or ornate. Streamlined arms may be made to hold cups and sockets for candles, or more elaborate arrangements, with floral motifs, or figurines can be constructed. We'll make a simple one first.

PHOTO SERIES 22
A candleholder

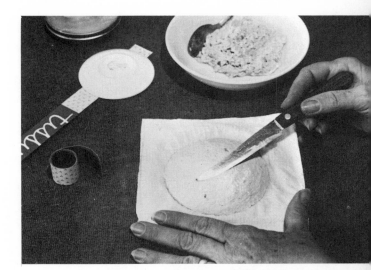

1. Forming the cups. Individual butter dishes are given a coating of petroleum jelly, then mash is pressed on the outside. A strip of light cardboard is rolled into a cylinder just the right size to hold a candle.

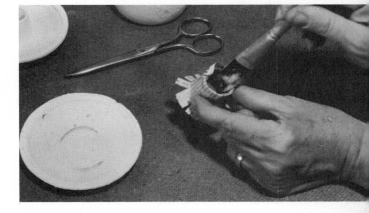

2. The socket is covered with newspaper and paste. Tabs are left at the bottom to help in fastening the socket in the cup.

3. A three-pronged candlestick is constructed. Long, slender, tapering supports have been rolled of white drawing paper. These are pasted on a mound that was formed by pressing mash over the end of a balloon. A piece of string holds the supports in position until the paste hardens.

When the supports were firmly fixed in place, the cups with candle sockets were attached at the ends with wads of bread paste.

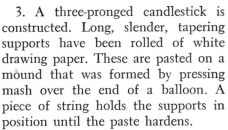

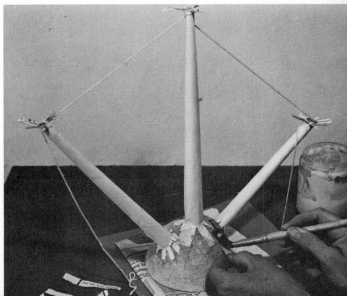

89

4. The completed candlestick. The flowers were cut out of light cardboard. Glue was brushed on both sides of the cutouts and, while the cardboard was damp, the petals were bent and curled. Bread paste was used to adhere the flowers to the candlestick base and also to adhere the center cutouts in each flower. String was dipped into glue and allowed to dry slightly, then it was curled and glued into place. Poster colors were used for the final painting and three coats of lacquer were sprayed on. The candle cups were painted with gold lacquer.

PHOTO SERIES 23
A flower girl candleholder

1. The body of the flower girl will be a cone, the head half a sphere. Two slender cones will form arms. At the left in the picture is the cone for the body. This was rolled from several layers of newspaper and paste, then kraft paper was pasted on. In the pan is a balloon, half of it covered with paper and paste. (Putting a balloon in a pan this way is a good way to hold it while paper is pasted on.) The half of the balloon showing was covered with five layers of newspaper and kraft paper. A slender cone is being rolled

and pasted to form one of the arms. In the lower left are two cups for candles made by pressing mash over butter dishes.

2. The head has been fastened at the apex of the cone, the two arms have been attached. Hands have been pressed out of mash and attached to the ends of the arms. For extra strength, pieces of coat hanger wire were cut and bent slightly and then inserted in the arms. The mash pressed for the hands covers the ends of wire that protrude slightly from the arms. The two cups with holders for candles are shown in the lower left.

3. Decorating. The entire work was given a base coat of white water-soluble wall paint, then the face was painted with water colors. A design was drawn on a strip of gold paper which was then pasted on the front of the figure. A strip of red ribbon was pasted at each side. Corded dress trim was dipped in gold lacquer and when dry was pasted around the back of the neck of the figure and down the sides of the front panel. A bit of red ribbon was glued around each wrist and a cuff of the gilded dress edging was glued in place next to the ribbon.

The cups have been given a coat of gold lacquer; these will be fastened to the hands with bread paste.

After the candle sockets were in place, the figurine was sprayed with three coats of lacquer. The inside of the head which is meant to hold flowers was given four extra coats of lacquer, brushed on, not sprayed. (Note: This treatment makes the inside of the head reasonably waterproof. However, when a bouquet is placed in the head, a small plastic bowl is placed inside the head to hold water.)

4. The candleholder in use.

91

Before we leave candleholders, we shall make one more, using a method of paper sculpture mentioned earlier—building a paper shell over a plastilene model.

1. A simplified bird form has been modeled in plastilene.

2. A layer of dampened newspaper is pasted over the model. This will be followed by a layer of brown kraft paper. The cup shape will serve as a crest and also as a socket to hold a candle.

3. Another layer of newspaper was pasted over the kraft layer and then the fourth layer of kraft paper was pasted over the newspaper. Here the final layer is being completed.

92

4. The shell has dried. It is cut in half with a sharp paring knife.

5. The two halves of the shell are removed from the model. Bits of plastilene remaining in the candle socket are dug out with a spoon handle.

6. The two empty portions of the shell are held together by rubber bands while strips of damp newspaper are pasted over the joint. For stability, the base of the candleholder should be weighted by gluing a stone inside before the two halves are joined.

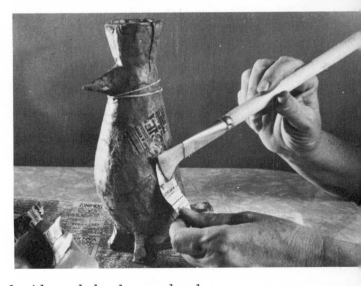

The finished bird can be decorated with cord, beads or colored paper. Here's a chance to use imagination. One way of decorating the bird is shown in color plate 30.

93

Trays of papier mâché are decorative and highly practical—light, but strong and durable.

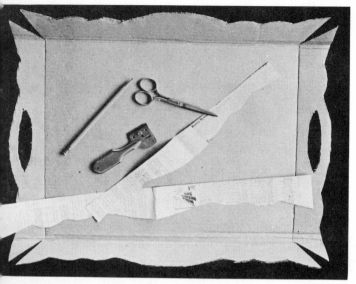

PHOTO SERIES 25
Trays

1. A pattern has been cut from a large piece of corrugated cardboard and scored on the lines along which it is to be folded.

2. The sides and the ends were folded up and fastened with cellophane tape; then the entire surface was covered with several layers of newspaper and paste. After the newspaper was dry, the tray was given a coat of gesso and a water color painting was mounted on it.

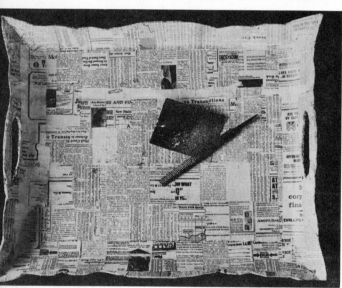

MOUNTING

The painting mounted on the tray was on paper so thin that paste could not be brushed on the back. Any moisture would have made the colors run. Before mounting, the painting was sprayed with fixative to give it a protective coating, then a generous layer of paste was brushed on a sheet of newspaper, covering an area larger than the painting. The painting, right side up, was laid on the layer of paste and gently patted with a paper napkin so that every portion of the back came into contact with the paste. The painting was then lifted up, placed on the tray and pressed firmly in place with a paper towel.

All portions of the tray not covered by the painting were painted with tempera colors. Then, when the work was thoroughly dry, it was given four coats of clear varnish. The finished tray is shown in color plate 33.

The pattern for the tray we just made was cut so that the sides flare outward. A tray with vertical sides can be made quite easily, merely by cutting the bottom portion out of a carton, leaving enough of the sides to provide a one inch rim for the tray, and extra height at the ends to allow handles to be cut.

3. The bottom portion of a carton is given a coating of newspaper and paste. (Note the handles at the ends.) When the pasting was completed and dry, the work was given a coat of gesso and decorated by montage. The outside edge was painted with a brilliant colored high-gloss enamel. Gold lacquer was painted on the top rim, after which the work was given four coats of clean varnish. The finished tray is shown in color plate 32.

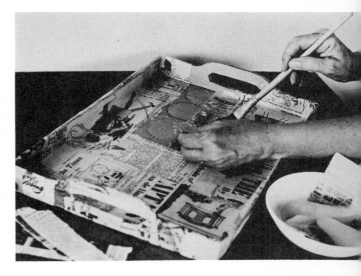

MONTAGE

The method of decoration used on this tray and on the cylinders in chapter 3 is well suited to papier mâché work. Montage need not be merely cutting out and pasting pictures; it offers highly creative possibilities when designs are made by pasting areas of paper of dif-

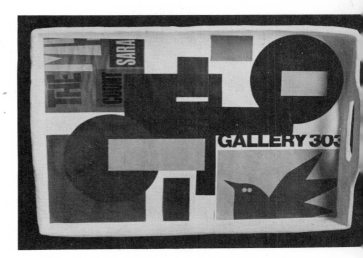

ferent colors or patterns juxtaposed and overlapped to form pleasing arrangements. Try a number of montages. The results are often unexpectedly exciting. A few exercises in this area will strengthen your feeling for design.

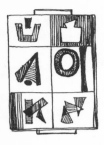

LAMPS

Papier mâché is an excellent material for making lamps. A lamp of conventional type in which a column supports a socket to hold a bulb and a lampshade holder can be made by building a papier mâché form over empty tin cans. Plate 20 shows the materials for

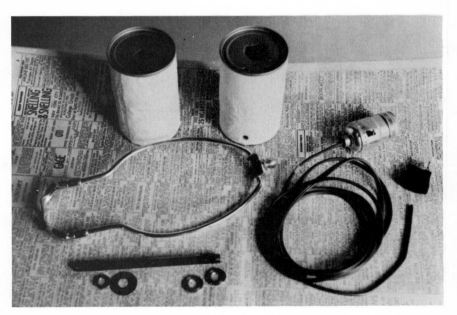

20. Materials for assembling a lamp

making such a lamp. Two empty tin cans have had paper glued on the sides. (This is so that paper can later be pasted on. Glue adheres to metal better than paste does.) The wiring fixtures for the lamp include a socket with switch (this has been attached to a length of wire); a brass loop to hold the lampshade (called a "harp"); a piece of metal tubing threaded on the outside (this tubing, made especially for lamps, has a thread that fits the socket); nuts and washers, and a plug to go on the other end of the wire. All these can be bought at an electrical supply store for $3.00 or less.

One of the tin cans has had a hole punched in the center of the top and another in the bottom. The other can has a hole in the top and one in the side near the bottom. The drawing shows how the wiring fixtures are assembled. After the assembly is completed, the two cans are fastened together with strips of paper and paste with the result shown in plate 21.

A lamp of this type can be finished and decorated by any of the methods shown for decorating cylinders in chapter 3. It can be covered

97

with a montage of colored papers, given a design with glued string, or given a smooth finish and then painted.

Even though we start with a cylindrical shape, the finished lamp need not be a cylinder. Forms can be built of paper mash to create rectangular shapes, vase forms or abstract designs as shown in the drawings.

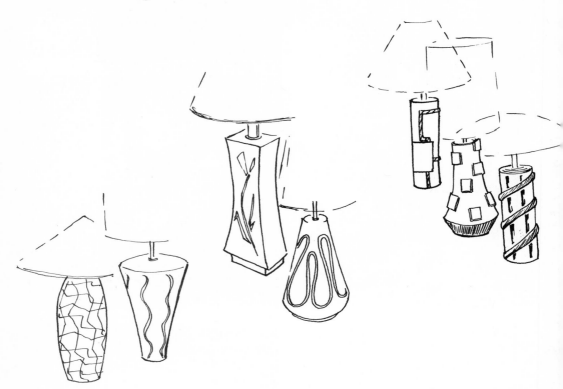

Papier mâché lamps can be made in less conventional shapes. Instead of having a column hold a bulb and a shade, a lamp can be designed so that the light shines through the form. Here is one way of doing this.

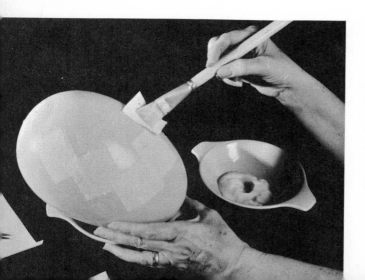

PHOTO SERIES 26
A lamp made over a balloon

1. Rectangles about two inches long cut from white paper toweling are pasted on a balloon. Care is taken to overlap the rectangles fairly evenly. Three layers of paper will be pasted on the balloon (glue should not be used in this step, since it is apt to make the paper stick fast to the balloon).

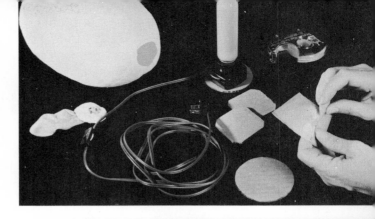

2. When the paper globe formed over the balloon was dry, an opening was cut at the bottom and the balloon was removed.

The lamp will require a base socket with wire and plug and a tubular bulb. A cord switch has been fastened on the wire.

A cardboard collar has been cut; it is being fastened with cellophane tape to form the base of the lamp. Cardboard circles will seal the bottom of the base. The cardboard squares are shims to raise the socket to the right height so that the bulb will be completely inside the globe.

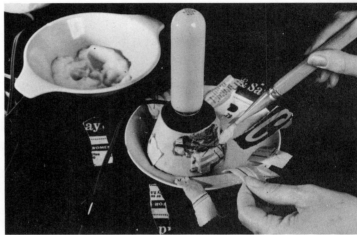

3. Completing the base. The two cardboard circles were glued together, the shims were glued on top of the circles, and the socket was glued on top of the shims. This assembly was then glued inside the collar. Pieces of newspaper are pasted on the surface of the collar. When the paper is dry, the base will be painted with black tempera color and given a coat of lacquer.

4. The finished lamp. The globe rests on the base without being fastened to it. Light shining through the overlapping rectangles of paper makes interesting patterns.

99

22. Globe lamp

23. Globe lamp

A variety of effects is attained by pasting arrangements of colored paper between the layers of paper toweling. These make designs which can be seen only when the lamp is turned on. Other things can be pasted between the layers—pieces of light twine, bits of fern, etc. There are many interesting things to try. Some experiments are shown in plates 22 and 23.

Lamps of other types may be made of papier mâché. For example, wall lamps with the bulb in back of a papier mâché shell give an indirect light. The shell can be an abstract form or a sculptural mask executed in paper. A pair of such masks is shown in the sketch. A lamp for a child's room can be designed as a doll's house with a light inside or as a friendly animal whose eyes glow in the dark. The opportunities for ingenuity and originality in designing papier mâché lamps are almost without limit.

100

A cocktail table of papier mâché, light, gay, practical, is an attractive addition to the furnishings of a modern interior.

The parts of a simply designed cocktail table are a circular top, a circular base, a vertical tubular column in two parts and a cone-shaped pedestal. The top and the base are each made of two circles cut from corrugated cardboard, glued together with a layer of pieces of corrugated cardboard in between. Thus both the top and the bottom are three layers thick. The edges are sealed with paper and glue. The vertical column is two cardboard cylinders, one larger in diameter than the other. The smaller cylinder is fastened to the top and the other to the bottom. The cone-shaped pedestal is rolled out of several sheets of newspaper. For extra stability, the lower portion of the cylinder attached to the base is weighted with stones.

The top of the table is covered with a layer of mash. When the table is assembled, the cone-shaped pedestal is attached to the underside of the top, then the cylinder that is fastened to the top is inserted into the cylinder attached to the bottom. Strips of paper and glue make the cone fast to the base. Next, mash is applied to the base and the pedestal, after which the construction of the table is completed.

Now that we have outlined the steps, let's watch the construction.

PHOTO SERIES 27
A cocktail table

1. Two circles 20 inches in diameter have been cut from pieces of cardboard. (Cardboard this large may be hard to find. Use the piece that forms the sides and bottom of a large carton or paste two pieces of cardboard together with strips of paper.)

A cardboard cylinder (the core of a roll of paper towels) is fastened in place in the center of a cardboard circle. A hole has been cut in the center of the other circle so that, when the top is assembled, this piece will slip over the column. Pieces of cardboard are glued to the underside of the top to form the layer between the two circles.

2. Binding the edge with newspaper and paste. Two complete bindings will be put around the edge, the second one of kraft paper. The two jars filled with water are weights. During the construction of the table top it must be kept under weights to prevent warping.

3. Completing the base. This was made in the same way as the top. The cylindrical column is a mailing tube, large enough in diameter so that the cylinder fastened to the top can slide into it.

4. The cylinder attached to the top is inserted in the one attached to the base (not fastened). The lower cylinder has been partly filled with stones so that the table top will be 19 inches above the floor. (The stones also add stability.)

5. Preparing the pedestal. Several sheets of newspaper have been rolled into a cone and fastened with paste. The cardboard circle with the edges cut and folded up and a hole cut in the center will be glued inside the cone.

102

6. Rolling a layer of mash for the table top. The mash is on a large sheet of plastic.

7. The table top was given a coating of glue, then placed upside down on the mash. The edge was also given a coating of glue. The layer of mash is being pressed against the edge of the table top.

8. Drying the top. After the mash was pressed against the top surface, the work was put upside down on several sheets of newspaper and heavily weighted with jars of water and bricks. The table top was allowed to remain under these weights until it was completely dry. This made the top surface true and level.

103

9. The construction of the top, the bottom and the pedestal has been completed. The top is shown in place but it is not yet fastened.

10. The pedestal is attached to the underside of the top. Strips of paper and paste are used to form a curve between the pedestal and the top.

11. Covering the pedestal with mash.

104

12. The three pieces of the table have been assembled. The pedestal is fastened to the base, and newspaper strips are used to make a curve where the pedestal and base join.

13. The construction of the table is complete. All areas have been covered with mash and allowed to dry. Rasp and sandpaper are used to smooth rough spots. After this, the entire work was given a coat of gesso.

The finished table is shown in color plate 39. It was decorated with cord and paint and gold lacquer. Three lines of cord were fastened to the edge of the top, twine was pasted on the pedestal to form diamond patterns, gold lacquer was used on the base, and the top edge. A chessboard painted on the top doubled the table's usefulness.

The construction we just made is entirely of paper except for the stones that weight the base. The work could have been simplified by using circles cut from ⅜-inch plywood for the top and the base, and a piece of 2-inch diameter wooden pole for the upright. All the wood could have been covered with paper, paste and mash.

What about using other materials this way? Is this cheating? Not at all. To the artist, any method or material which achieves the desired result is proper to use. A wooden frame completely covered with paper and mash is a legitimate article of papier mâché.

Many other decorative and useful articles of furniture can be made of papier mâché—wall cabinets with shelves, linen chests, toy boxes for a child's room. Don't hesitate to use pieces of discarded wooden packing cases when doing so would help to speed the construction or make the articles stronger.

Little skill in carpentry is required and special woodworking tools are unnecessary. Aside from sawing a piece of wood or two and hammering a few nails, all the work is done with paper, paste and glue.

Decorating such articles can be an exciting experience. Ornaments can be built up of mash, flat areas can be painted with abstract designs, patterns can be outlined in heavy cord which is glued on. There are practically no limitations. Experiment. Be bold.

11
PAPIER
MÂCHÉ
ON
STAGE

A different kind of interior decor is used by those masters of illusion and merchants of make-believe—the theater set designers. Since stage settings are temporary things and props must be light, inexpensive, and expendable, what better material for their construction than papier mâché?

Plate 24 shows a "magic" mask, 26 inches tall, built of cardboard, paper and paste, used in a production of *Bell, Book and Candle*. Parts of the mask are covered with aluminum foil. The earrings were cut from heavy aluminum foil (throw-away pie plates). In the course of the play this mask had to be broken. (In theatrical parlance, such a prop is called a "break-away.") Plate 25 shows the broken mask. A few strips of paper and paste on the back put it together again in perfect shape for the next performance.

107

24. "Magic" mask,
stage prop

25. "Magic" mask
broken

26. Drawing, stage prop for *Bell, Book and Candle*

Plate 26 shows a framed drawing, another prop for *Bell, Book and Candle*. The action of the play required the drawing of a dancer to hang on a wall. The wall in this case was a piece of canvas, so the drawing and its frame had to be almost weightless. This frame was made of newspaper rolled into tubes 1 inch in diameter, mitered at the corners. It was painted with black poster color, then strokes of gold lacquer were roughly brushed over the surface.

Plate 27 shows a larger framed picture used in a production of *Never Too Late*. The frame was made of corrugated cardboard and

109

27. Painting, stage prop for *Never Too Late*

rolls of newspaper. The ornate character of this frame provided the rococo note called for by the set designer.

For a production of *The Waltz of the Toreadors*, two special props were needed, one of them a shield holding two swords. The swords were Navy dress swords lent by a member of the company. The shield was constructed as follows.

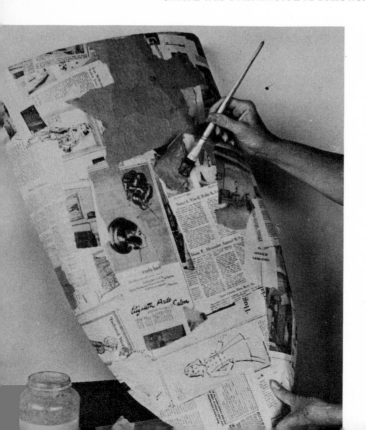

PHOTO SERIES 28
A *shield*

1. The outline of a shield 30 inches tall was cut from corrugated cardboard. The cardboard was curved and held in this shape by heavy cord while newspaper was pasted over both sides. When the paper dried, the shield retained its curved form. Slots were cut in the edges of the shield to receive the swords.

110

2. The finished shield with swords in place. The shield was not painted, but decorated with colored paper. The lions are gold, mounted on a red field; the fleurs de lis are white on a royal blue background.

111

The other prop used in the same play was a support for a canopy over the head of a bed. The set designer required something ornate 34 inches high. Here is the way it was built.

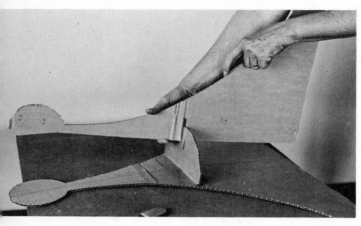

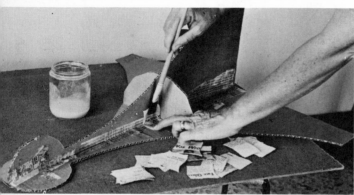

1. A framework is built of shapes cut from corrugated cardboard.

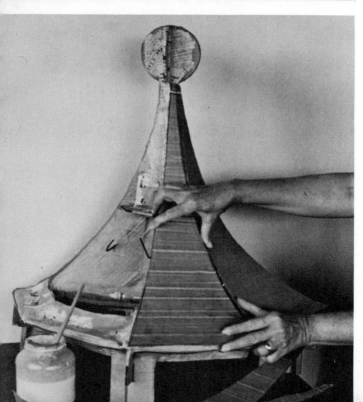

2. The front rib is fastened against the back.

3. Curved side panels are fastened in place. Before this was done, hooks made of a heavy coat hanger wire were fastened against the back. These hooks are to hold the drapery (at left in photo). A loop of the same wire was fastened at the back of the construction to hold the canopy support against the wall.

112

4. Curved side panels are covered with newspaper and paste.

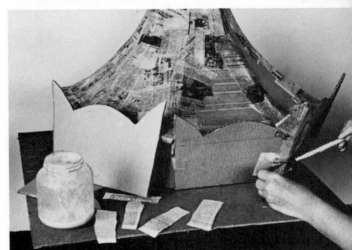

5. Crown-shaped edge panels are fastened in place with newspaper.

6. Newspaper has been crumpled to make a ball at the top. The newspaper is held in place by a rubber band while strips of paper are pasted on the ball.

113

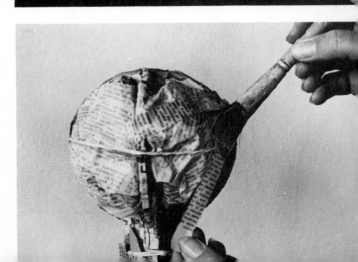

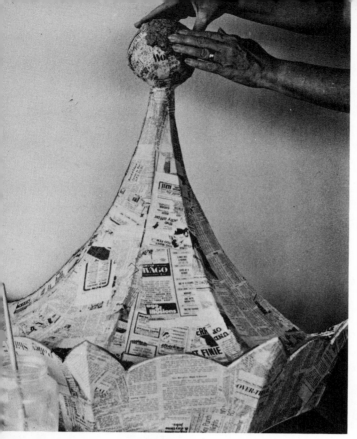

7. The ball at the top has dried. Now mash is pressed on to complete the spherical shape. The rest of the construction has been covered with newspaper.

8. One coat of gold lacquer was brushed over the entire construction. At this point, it was decided to make the piece more ornate. Heavy cord dipped in glue was fastened to the edge panels as shown. This cord had to be pinned in place while the glue hardened.

9. The finished canopy support.

Masks with more detail than the one shown in plate 24, or requiring more resemblance to human features, can be made by modeling the face in plastilene, then covering the model with three layers of damp paper (torn into small pieces) and paste. The first layer of paper should be newspaper, the second layer, kraft paper, and the third, white toilet tissue. Paper can be put directly on the plastilene with no danger of it sticking fast. When the paper shell is dry, it can be easily lifted off the model. A few undercuts don't matter, for plastilene remains soft and any bits that get caught in the mask can be dug out.

Marionette heads can be made by the same method. In this case, a model of a complete head must be made in plastilene and supported on an armature. Layers of paper and paste are built up over the entire head. When the shell has dried, it is cut in half with a razor blade, the plastilene is removed from the inside, and the two empty shells are held together while the joint is sealed with paper and paste. (This was illustrated in photo series 24.)

Puppetry is an important art form and many books have been written about it. We cannot attempt to cover the subject here except to point out that a craftsman skilled in papier mâché can construct almost any accessory required for a marionette theater as well as many of the props needed for a full-sized stage.

115

12

PATIO

SCULPTURE

Thenings we have made up to this point have all been for indoor use. Now, let us consider sculpture suitable for a patio or a garden.

Where there is a roof over a portion of a patio, papier mâché that has been given several protective coatings of varnish can remain outdoors. If it is not exposed to a drenching rain, it will not be harmed by the occasional spatterings of showers.

The female figure shown in color plates 45, 46, and 47 is an amusing patio accessory. She sits in on parties, lifts her glass with the guests and, with her changes of wigs and jewelry, enters into the spirit of any social gathering. She was made as follows:

1. A large paper bag stuffed with crumpled newspaper has been tied in the middle for a waist and at the top for a neck. Arms and legs are rolls of newspaper; the head is a balloon with paper pasted on the surface.

The figure was constructed by the method shown in photo series 10 and 11. Strips of newspaper were pasted, folded lengthwise and then wrapped around the body, the arms and the legs—building up anatomical detail.

2. The basic construction of the body, neck and limbs has been almost completed. The hands and feet are still crumpled newspaper.

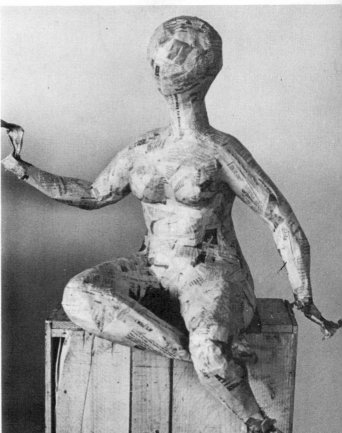

3. Making a hand. Five slender tubes of newspaper are rolled to serve as fingers. The tubes are fastened at one end with a rubber band and this portion is inserted into the arm at what will be the wrist.

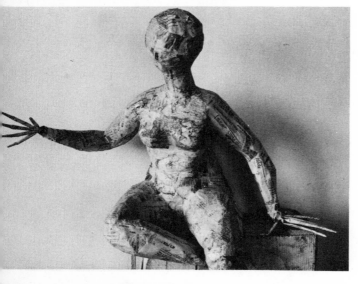

4. Two hands have been roughly constructed and are in place. Pieces of coat hanger wire were cut to the proper length and inserted in all of the fingers and the thumbs.

5. Modeling on the hands and the feet has been carried further.

118

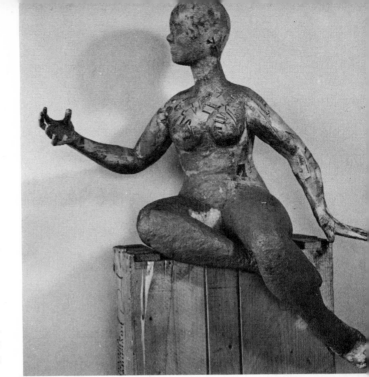

6. Modeling is nearly finished. Mash has been pressed on the lower limbs and parts of the torso. Facial features have been modeled in mash.

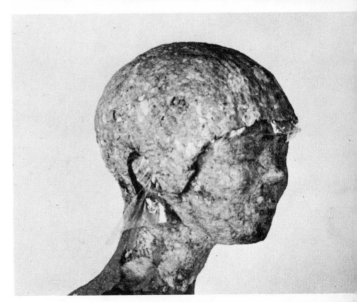

7. Construction of a wig. The head has been covered with a thin sheet of plastic (sandwich wrapping). A coiffure has been constructed of paper, paste and mash. The plastic will make it possible to lift off the wig.

8. Construction of the body has been completed. The entire figure was given a coating of spackle. After the spackle dried, the figure was sandpapered. A second wig with a different type of hairdo is in place.

119

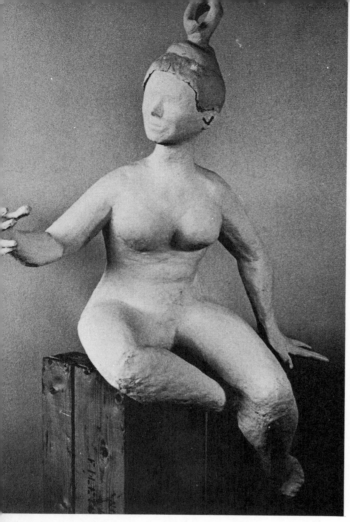

9. The work has been painted with one coat of water-base acrylic wall paint. A little dry, powdered red pigment was mixed in to produce a pink approximating that of flesh color. The pink was toned down by adding a little yellow, a touch of green and a touch of black casein color. The figure wears a third wig of a different style. The ears have been pierced so that she may wear papier mâché earrings. Match sticks have been stuck through the ear holes so that they will not be filled with paint.

10. The finished figure wearing a bikini (also made of paper) and a pair of papier mâché earrings.

120

11. Another version, a different wig and false eyelashes. A third wig is shown in color plate 45.

The mermaid shown in color plate 41 has hung on an outdoor patio for several years. She is just as bright and colorful today as the day she was made. (She is 8 feet, 4 inches long.)

An architectural decoration suitable for any wall, but ideal for a masonry wall in a patio can be made of papier mâché in the same manner as the fish pressed in a mold in chapter 8. The steps are the same, the only difference being that the product is larger.

PHOTO SERIES 31
A mural

1. Units of an imaginative scene are modeled in plastilene.

2. The parts of the city-scape have been completed and assembled on a glass table top. (Newspaper is under the glass.) A mold of the scene will be made by pouring plaster over the model. (It is not necessary to cover the glass with petroleum jelly because plaster can be poured on glass and, after it sets, can be lifted off easily.)

Care must be taken to press the plastilene firmly against the glass and to check the model to see that there are no undercuts.

A retaining wall to hold the plaster has been built of clay. (Plastilene could have been used for the retaining wall. We just happened to have a quantity of clay on hand which has been used for plaster casting. We keep it moist in a plastic bag and use it over and over again for this type of work.)

3. Pouring plaster. Plaster of Paris was sprinkled into water until a mound showed above the surface. This indicated that enough plaster had been used. When the plaster sank into the water, the mixture was stirred for two minutes before pouring.

This bowlful will not be sufficient to make the complete mold, but just enough to cover the plastilene model. After it was poured, the plaster was blown upon to make sure there were no bubbles against the model. Then another batch of plaster, large enough to make the mold one inch thick, was mixed and poured. (A fresh batch of plaster can be poured on top of one previously poured, provided the latter has not become dry.)

4. The mold has set; the plastilene model is being removed. After this the mold must be examined for undercuts. If there are any, the edges of the depressions must be trimmed with a knife so that no undercuts remain.

The mold must be allowed to dry completely—a process which may take several days. The drying can be hastened by putting the mold in strong sunlight and, after dark, exposing it to the rays of an electric heater.

5. Pressing. The mold is dry. Petroleum jelly has been brushed on the surface and into all of the depressions; then the excess was wiped off with paper towels. Paper pulp (with nothing added) is pressed into the recesses of the mold. In this pressing, only the plastilene model was reproduced in papier mâché.

6. The pressing was allowed to dry twenty-four hours, then removed from the mold. It is almost impossible to remove a delicate, complicated shape like this in one piece, but this is not a serious problem. (It was expected that the pressing would break at the narrow portions). The pieces of the pressing have been assembled and glued in place on a large piece of kraft paper. The surface of the design is brushed with diluted glue. Later, when the glue had set, the kraft paper was trimmed away from the edges of the design.

7. The mural in place, glued onto a patio wall in a spot where it catches the rays of the morning sun.

8. A second pressing made with a background of papier mâché is shown in color plate 42. This is a movable bas-relief plaque 20 inches by 28 inches.

123

The plaque we just made is about the maximum size that can be pressed in a single mold. A larger mural can be made by planning the design so that it may be modeled in sections with separate molds cast for each piece. The pressings are assembled on the wall into a single unit. The only limitation on the size of such a mural is the area of the wall it is to adorn.

Something in an entirely different vein is shown in the next series.

PHOTO SERIES 32
Abstract garden sculpture

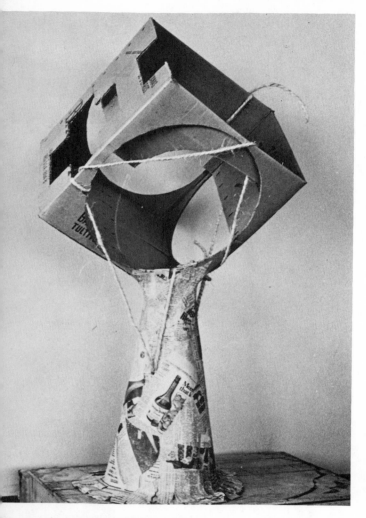

1. A cardboard carton with openings of different shapes cut in its sides has been fastened to a cone rolled from sheets of newspaper. Cord holds the carton and the cone together while the pasted joint between them hardens.

2. The surface of the carton is being covered with a layer of newspaper and paste.

124

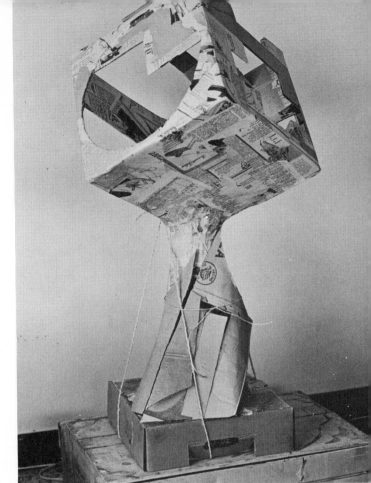

3. Pieces of cardboard are used to change the contour of the cone.

4. Newspaper has been pasted over the added cardboard.

125

5. The contour of the supporting column has been changed, height has been added at the base; another element cut from cardboard has been added to the design at the top. The lower portion of the construction has been covered with mash.

6. The completed sculpture. Another carton was added to the base to form a rectangular pedestal. (The carton was weighted with stones.) The entire work was covered with mash, then given a coat of spackle and glue. When the spackle was thoroughly dry, it was sprayed with several coats of lacquer.

7. Another view.

8. Another view.

127

The abstract sculpture whose making we have just watched has given a great deal of pleasure in a garden. The intricate interlocking of forms creates a constantly changing pattern of light and shade as the sun moves overhead. The work is 54 inches tall yet, despite the fact that the base is weighted, it is light enough to be carried easily. Thus it can be moved from place to place in the garden or in the patio. When night falls or inclement weather threatens, it is brought indoors.

The piece of sculpture, an abstract head, shown in plate 28 hanging on a patio wall, also provides changing patterns of light and shade. Plate 29 shows it on a wall in a garden. This, too, is brought indoors at nightfall.

Does an artist know what he is going to do before he does it? Not always. Not exactly, that is. Usually when he starts out to create something, he has a pretty good idea of what it is to be, but somewhere along the line changes are bound to take place. As work progresses, rhythms and relationships between parts are more clearly seen and often there is a need for alterations in the original concept. The material enters into the creative process also, making its own contribution to the design.

And so, the final product may be different from what it started out to be. And that is good, for sculpture must really grow under the artist's hands.

28. A semi-abstract head, hanging on a patio wall

29. Sculpture on a wall in a garden

129

13
MORE
ABOUT
MATERIALS

Papier mâché is twenty centuries old but it is still a young art. No technical library has been written about it. Those who explore the possibilities of this medium proceed by trial and error, learning as they go along.

Recent developments in the field of synthetics have made many more materials available—glues, pigments, varnishes. Some of these are a great boon to the artist in papier mâché, but their great profusion is sometimes a bit confusing. Where there are so many to choose from, how can one select wisely?

We have made more than five hundred experiments, trying different methods of paper construction, testing recipes for mash, comparing pigments, lacquers and varnishes. The methods and the materials described in previous chapters are those which we have found work best. But they are not the only ones that may be used.

The following is a brief summary of materials available to the artist who works in papier mâché.

Paper

The important material, of course, is paper—paper of all kinds. But other materials can be used also—cloth for draping, coat hanger wire for hooks and for reinforcement, cord for decoration. We have seen how basic forms can be built out of paper; we have seen, too, how constructions can be made on things which already exist—tin cans, for example, and cardboard containers. When time can be saved by using such aids, the artist uses them, and the product is just as creative and original and as truly papier mâché as if every bit of it had been fashioned entirely from paper mash. The possibilities of using such things as cigar boxes, mushroom baskets and round wooden cheese boxes as frames to build on should not be overlooked.

Styrofoam makes a good base material for papier mâché. It is light, easily carved and inexpensive. It can be bought in blocks or in special shapes, such as balls, cones, egg shapes, that are especially useful in some types of construction.

Paste and glue

When should one use paste, when should one use glue? This is a matter of individual preference. Paste takes longer to dry and makes a somewhat softer product. Most artists use paste for building basic forms; when paper is applied with the fingers instead of a brush, paper strips are soaked in a diluted mixture of paste and glue.

As we said in chapter 1, we have found wheat paste, the type used to hang wallpaper, best for paper construction. But we promised to give a recipe for those who want to make their own paste. Here it is:

Paste is made by mixing flour with a little water, then slowly adding more water to make a thin, milky consistency, then heating with constant stirring until the batch thickens. Another method is the following:

Bring two cups of water to a boil, mix ½ cup of flour and cold water to the consistency of thin cream. Pour this slowly into the boiling water and stir until the paste is thick. A few drops of oil of cloves or oil of wintergreen may be added as a preservative.

Among all the glues available, the best in our opinion is the white synthetic glue that comes in liquid form in plastic containers. When this glue is used full strength, it hardens rapidly with a tough surface. Glue is better than paste for fastening paper to wood or metal or for attaching details at the end of a construction. White glue brushed over a papier mâché object serves as an excellent sealer, filling pores, adding strength and providing a good surface to paint on.

131

Powdered casein glue which must be mixed with water is a hard adhesive, good for woodworking. When used on paper, it makes the finished product somewhat brittle. This glue must be mixed in small quantities because it spoils after a day or two. (Casein is made from refined curd of milk.)

Epoxy, an extremely strong adhesive, is recommended by some papier mâché artists not only as a glue but as a final coating in place of varnish. Epoxy comes in two containers, the contents of which must be mixed together before the glue is ready for use. Epoxy sets with a hard, glossy surface; when applied to paper surfaces it makes them almost completely impervious to liquids.

We have found epoxy difficult to use in papier mâché work. It cannot be brushed on easily and it is hard to spread evenly over a surface. It must be handled with extreme caution because it can harm the skin or the eyes. Safety directions on the containers must be followed carefully.

Starch

Some artists use liquid starch as an adhesive, especially when draping. We have found that paste and glue work better, but you may wish to experiment.

Rubber cement

This is used by commercial artists for mounting drawings on cardboard. A coating of cement is applied to the back of the drawing and another coating is applied to the cardboard. Both coats are allowed to dry, then the drawing is put into position and firmly pressed into place. Rubber cement is useful in making montages.

PRIMERS

Water-base paints

Paint can be applied to paper constructions after they have dried. Colors with a water base sink into the paper and this often gives a pleasing effect. In most cases, however, it is advisable to give the work a base or priming coat before colors or decorations are brushed on. One of the most satisfactory materials for a base coat is synthetic water-base wall paint sold under various trade names. Two coats of this brushed on papier mâché with a twenty-four hour interval allowed between coats provide an excellent surface for further painting and decorating.

Gesso

When some form of calcium such as chalk, whiting or plaster of Paris is mixed with glue, the result is a plastic material which can be

132

used as a surface coating prior to painting. This mixture is called gesso. When it dries, it can be sandpapered to a smooth ivory-like finish. (The less glue used, the easier the surface is to sandpaper.) Some recipes for gesso call for linseed oil, others omit this ingredient. We have found that a small amount of oil makes gesso easier to work with. (See recipe in chapter 2.)

A prepared gesso made of acrylic polymer latex emulsion can be bought in ready-to-use form. We have tried this and, while it is satisfactory, we have found better results with the gesso we mix ourselves.

Spackle

This material is used for patching plaster walls. When mixed with water into a thick paste, it can be modeled almost like modeling clay. When more water is added, it can be applied with a brush. A small quantity of glue added to the water makes it a kind of gesso.

Linseed oil

We know this material as an extender for pigments and as an ingredient of mash. It also makes a good base coat for papier mâché. Three or four successive coats of linseed oil brushed over dry mash give it a tough surface and make it water resistant. Objects that have been coated with linseed oil, then baked in the oven until the surface starts to turn brown, become quite tough and almost impervious to water.

Linseed oil can be purchased raw or boiled. The former is lighter in color and is better for pieces which are to be painted white. Where whiteness is not important, either may be used.

Synthetic primers

Art supply dealers sell a variety of specially prepared priming compounds. These are used to size canvas for oil painting, but many of them can be used on papier mâché. The directions on the containers tell when they are suitable for use on paper.

As we mentioned earlier, white synthetic glue used either full strength or diluted with water is an excellent primer, probably the most convenient for the papier mâché artist.

Paints

Water colors

The entire range of paints and pigments available for art work can be used for papier mâché. Probably the easiest to handle (and the least expensive) are opaque water colors—tempera, poster colors.

Transparent water colors are good where gradations and shading of tone are required. Transparent colors can be mixed with bread paste

133

Porcelain-like finish

Some papier mâché articles have portions so smooth and glossy that they resemble porcelain. To achieve this effect, the article must be pressed in a mold or worked on with fine sandpaper. The surface can be given two or three base coats of either water-base wall paint or gesso with some sandpapering in between coats if necessary. After the wall paint or gesso has dried, it should be brushed with diluted white glue. When this has dried, decorations may be painted on, then the work should be sprayed with fixative, then another coat of diluted glue should be brushed on (the fixative prevents the colors from smearing). When the last coat of glue is thoroughly dry, a final coat of clear varnish, clear lacquer or fast-drying clear enamel should be brushed on. (Varnish and lacquer give the work a tint resembling that of old ivory; clear enamel is colorless.)

Antiquing

This term is applied to a method of treating surfaces by putting a darker pigment on, then wiping most of it off. The darker pigment stays in surface crevices and so accentuates the texture. The use of milk and instant coffee for antiquing was illustrated in chapter 1. Walnut varnish thinned with turpentine produces a similar effect. Some artists use a bit of tar dipped in lacquer thinner and dragged over the work, or a dark brown oil paint (burnt sienna, burnt umber) thinned with turpentine.

Wax

Products made for waxing furniture or automobiles can be used on papier mâché. Colors that come in "rub-on" wax form (used by ceramists on bisque or greenware) give interesting effects when applied to papier mâché that has been given a base coat of gesso or acrylic white. "Antique" colors in rub-on wax form can also be used.

CARE OF BRUSHES

The pleasure of painting is greater if one has good brushes and takes care of them. Painting should be done with the forward portion of the brush. Try not to dip the brush so far into the paint that it gets on the ferrule. Paint that gets into the roots of the hairs is almost impossible to remove, and when it cakes there, it lowers the effectiveness of the brush.

When painting is finished, brushes should be wiped, then rinsed in whatever solvent is used for the paint—water for water colors, turpentine for oil paints and varnishes, alcohol for shellac, and thinner for lacquers. The container the paint comes in will tell what solvent should be used.

After rinsing, brushes should be washed with soap and warm running water. When all of the soap has been rinsed out, brushes should be "dressed," that is, gently squeezed and shaped with the fingers, then put aside to dry.

In papier mâché there is no one best way of doing anything and there is no single material that is just right for all occasions. As you make more objects in this medium, you will find the materials and the methods that you like best and the tools that are most comfortable in your hands. You will develop special techniques, devise your own recipes. And, like all other artists in papier mâché, you will continue to try out the new.

14
THE ART
OF
PAPIER
MÂCHÉ

WE have covered a lot of ground together, been through a number of projects, made things large and small. By this time we have acquired the skills of papier mâché and have learned to love the material.

After techniques have been mastered, the next problems become: What shall we make? How do we arrive at good design? What rules must we follow?

There are no rules for creating a work of art—there can't be. We must find our own guideposts. In designing ability, as in manual skill, we grow through practice. The more objects we make, the better we become at making them; the more planning we do, the better our planning becomes. As we design, our designs grow in strength and originality.

Drawing helps. Keep a sketch book. Make many, many sketches. Whenever an idea for a form or a pattern occurs to you, jot it down. Draw objects from nature. Sketch people, animals, flowers, fruits. Sketch coffee pots, pitchers, cracker boxes, cups and saucers, vases.

Doodle. Put pencil to paper and let it wander. Draw abstract shapes. Keep these in the sketch book and, after time has passed, look at them again; they may suggest ideas for things to create of paper. Out of doodles often grow original works of art.

Do some exercises in design. How many ways can a candlestick be planned? Make a series of drawings (at least twelve). Use some shapes of people, make some of the designs abstract.

Another exercise in design: see how many ways you can divide up the area of a square. Start with a square 4 inches on a side (or a rectangle or a circle), divide the space within geometrically with circles and radial lines. Fill adjacent spaces with contrasting colors.

Still another exercise to try: select some motif such as a flower or a bird (a rooster is good), and see how many ways this motif can be used to fill the area of a rectangle or a circle.

Doodle in three dimensions. Make sketches out of moistened newspaper squeezed into odd shapes. Cut strips of cardboard, fold them and join them in different ways. Model in mash. See what completely new forms develop.

What shall we make? Anything you wish, but keep function in mind. Make of papier mâché the things papier mâché makes best. It does not hold liquids well, so leave the making of bowls and pots to the potters. But for some things papier mâché is just right, better in fact than any other material. A large wall plaque of papier mâché can hang where a ceramic plaque would be too heavy. (If papier mâché falls, it rarely breaks and when it does, it is easy to repair.)

What about taste? We all like to do things that will be considered in good taste, yet taste is a hard quality to define. It is such a personal thing; one person's good taste is another's horrible example. We must have the courage to do what we believe in, to make the things we like without fear of what people may say. One of the greatest values of papier mâché is the almost total lack of value of the things that go into its making. Papier mâché jewelry, for example, is not made of gold and its sparkle comes from bits of colored glass. It is gaudy and its gaudiness is its virtue. No need for restraint; the most startling patterns, the strongest colors—these in papier mâché are good taste.

The criticism we must heed is our own. As we work, we develop in appreciation of what is good. It is inevitable that some of the things we make will not turn out as we planned. They may be good (the happy accidents artists love). They may be bad; in that case we must have the courage to destroy them.

How about selling the things we make? Wonderful idea. Numbers of artists in papier mâché have been able to combine a delightful,

139

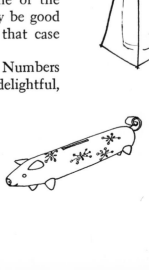

creative activity with a profitable business enterprise. Department stores, gift shops, art galleries, are eager to deal in products that are beautiful and original. The idea is worth looking into.

Finally, we must constantly explore, try new ideas, new ways. We must be bold. Whatever we make, be it for use or for decoration, its greatest value is the joy it brings to us as we make it.

To build something, to watch it grow, take form, acquire color, therein lies the deep satisfaction that leads to happiness.

INDEX

141

143

About the Authors

JOHN B. KENNY is well known to artists everywhere for his three books, *The Complete Book of Pottery Making, Ceramic Sculpture* and *Ceramic Design.*

The enormous success of these books, their adoption by a large number of schools, colleges and universities, as well as by artists and craftsmen, is due to the author's wide background as a skilled potter and experienced teacher. For over twenty years Mr. Kenny was principal of the High School of Art and Design, New York City's specialized high school for preparing young people for professional careers as artists and designers.

Examples of Mr. Kenny's work are included in private collections in this country and in Europe. He holds the degree of Master of Fine Arts in ceramics from Alfred University and is a member of the Society of Illustrators.

CARLA KENNY, an illustrator of note in her own right and also a member of the Society of Illustrators, did illustrations for John Kenny's *Ceramic Design.* This is her first collaboration in writing a book with Mr. Kenny.

John and Carla Kenny and their daughter, Pamela, live in Cuernavaca, Mexico.